POWER AND *ANOINTING* NEEDED FOR...

KINGDOM INTERCESSION

...To Rend the Heavens...

...FOR THE KINGDOM OF HEAVEN TO COME ON EARTH AS IT IS IN HEAVEN

"Put on the whole armour of God, that ye may be able to stand against the wiles of the devil." Eph. 6:11

Dr. Pernell H. Hewing, Ph.D., Th.D.

Copyright © 2012 by Pernell H. Hewing
921 W. Main St., Whitewater, WI 53190
All rights reserved

*POWER AND ANOINTING NEEDED
FOR KINGDOM INTERCESSOR*

Sanctuary Word Press

Pernell H. Hewing, Ph.D., Th.D.
921 W. Main Street
Whitewater, Wisconsin 53190-1706
(262) 473-7472   Fax (262) 473-9724
www.thesanctuarywhitewater.com

This publication is a tool to teach, to train, and to inform Christians, and also to minister and lead Christians into a deep ministry of God's Word and Work.

All rights reserved. No part of this publication may be reproduced or transmitted in any form or by any means electronic or mechanical, including photocopying, recording or any information storage and retrieval system, without permission in writing from the publisher.

Scripture quotations are from the King James Bible © 1917, 1929, 1934, 1957, 1964, 1982, and 1988 by the B.B. KIRKBRIDE BIBLE COMPANY, INC.

For additional information about
Sanctuary Word Press,

Call (262) 473-7472

First Printing: 2012

POWER AND *ANOINTING* NEEDED FOR...

KINGDOM INTERCESSION

...To Rend the Heavens

TO OPEN THE WAY...
            ...FOR THE KING TO COME

"For we wrestle not against flesh and blood, but against principalities, against powers, against the rulers of the darkness of this world, against spiritual wickedness in high places." Ephesians 6:12

Dr. Pernell H. Hewing, Ph.D., Th.D.

**The Lord says Come enter into...
The Ministry of *Kingdom Intercession*...**

... to prepare to rend the Heaven and open the way for the Kingdom of Heaven to come on earth as it is in heaven.

It is written...

"And Jesus called a little child unto him, and set him in the midst of them,

"And said, Verily I say unto you, Except ye be converted, and become as little children, ye shall not enter into the Kingdom of Heaven.

"Whosoever therefore shall humble himself as this little child, the same is greatest in the Kingdom of Heaven."
Matthew 18:2-4

PREFACE

Prepare yourself for an unusual journey if you answer the call to the ministry of **Kingdom Intercession**. You will get a panoramic view of the *Kingdom of Heaven* and what is required to be prepared to serve in the *Royal Priesthood*. It is a ministry of prayer, travail, and intercession open to every born-again believer of the Lord Jesus Christ.

This book introduces the call to a higher level of intercession and to the ministry of the call to a higher level of prayer coupled with intercession for a most strategic purpose—to open the way for the Kingdom of Heaven to invade the Church and for the born again to enter into the call to live and move in the Kingdom of Heaven on earth. It is a call to open the way for the King of kings and Lord of lords to come into the Church and to invade the ministry of the Church.

The Ministry of **Kingdom Intercession** is a special ministry to prepare for entrance into the Kingdom of Heaven on earth. It brings into focus God's ways of dealing with mankind, and how He establishes His plan and purposes for the Church and with mankind. It takes one back to the first church in the wilderness and to the Levitical Ministry of the Old Testament.

The ministry of the Levite is a ministry that is not dead, but a ministry waiting to be revealed in the New Testament End-time Church through the Royal Priesthood. There is an urgent call in this end-time age for the restoration of the Priesthood Ministry. This is the ministry of **Kingdom Intercession**, which is a ministry for which much preparation is needed--preparation before the Lord God Almighty. It is a ministry to prepare believers to live out the Kingdom of Heaven on earth.

One's journey in preparation for this ministry of **Kingdom Intercession** will lead along a pathway to the place where Levites paid the price for their awesome privileged call to serve in the Priesthood. The hope is that the born-again will lodge here until he/she decides to pay the same price the Levites of old paid for their call to serve in the *Royal Priesthood* in the Kingdom of Heaven.

The one who accepts this call will cascade back and forth across the pages of the Bible treading uncharted waters in prayer and intercession and being pushed on to deeper prayer and higher intercession in and for the New Testament Church. This call to **Kingdom Intercession** is a significant call to ministers. It will take the one who accepts this call beyond what one knows now as ministry and ministering in and for the New Testament Church. It leads ministers to the call to enter into the Kingdom of Heaven as revealed in the book of Matthew and on to becoming Kings and Priests unto God the Father by Jesus Christ.

It is written...

"And from Jesus Christ, who is the faithful witness, and the first begotten of the dead, and the prince of the kings of the earth. Unto him that loved us, and washed us from our sins in his own blood,

*"And hath made us kings and priests unto God and his Father; to him be glory and dominion for ever and ever."
Revelations 1:5-6*

As one enters into the ministry of **Kingdom Intercession**, he/she will be led along a pathway to unconditional surrender. To be a Levite of the Old Testament, there was no other way but unconditional surrender for the Levites had charge of the temple service and stood for the congregation. The **Kingdom Intercessor** must live life as the Levites of the Old Testament—a life totally sold out to God.

The **Kingdom Intercessor** of the New Testament Church will be positioned in the Church as the Royal Priest. That one must be liberated from the world, from self, and from the wiles of the enemy in order to live, move and serve in the Kingdom of Heaven.

The New Testament **Kingdom Intercessor** will be given an opportunity to look into the Kingdom of Heaven requirements. Kingdom of Heaven requirements are the requirements that earn for one Levitical credentials. Levitical credentials are Royal Priesthood credentials and they open the way for one's **Priestly** Place in Kingdom work.

Finally, the King calls, "Come, Beloved, let us enter into this place of rest and service for the Lord." The practical aspects of this call is to the one saying yes to this call is to read, study and complete the practical exercises in this book to ensure one's Royal Priesthood position in the Kingdom of Heaven.

Pernell H. Hewing, Ph.D., Th.D.

Special Note from the Author

This book is written to prepare Kingdom Intercessors to open the way for the Kingdom to come on earth as it is in Heaven.

Since Kingdom Intercession is orchestrated by God, and some have not understood and/or have not completed the requirements for preparation, this book can be used by training schools, prayer ministries, churches or as a school of ministry training which can be completed at home.

For independent study, several special books by this author are suggested at the end of various sections in this book for deeper understanding.

Additional books by this author which will be helpful for this training are described in the list at the end of this book along with ordering information.

Table of Contents

Preface 9

PART I: CALLING FORTH INTERCESSORS TO PREPARE FOR *KINGDOM INTERCESSION* 11

Chapter 1
Kingdom Intercession, the Vanguard for the Kingdom of Heaven to Invade the Earth 13

Chapter 2
Special *Anointing* and Power of the Believer's Prayer 23

Chapter 3
The Higher Realm of Prayer Power 31

PART II: THE CALL TO *KINGDOM INTERCESSION* .. 37

Chapter 4
Preparation for the Ministry of *Kingdom Intercession* 39

Chapter 5
The Intercessor is Adorned with Kingdom Garments 47

Chapter 6
The King Comes to Prepare the Intercessor For the Kingdom 53

Chapter 7
    The Intercessor, Prepared and Ready for
    Kingdom Intercession   65

Chapter 8
    The *Kingdom Intercessor* is a "Hidden One"   71

Chapter 9
    The Call Now is Personal. Will You Answer?.   81

PART III: *KINGDOM INTERCESSOR* **CALLED TO THE**
    FRONTLINE OF THE BATTLE FOR CONTROL. 93

Chapter 10
    The *Kingdom Intercessor* Called to
    Stratospheric Warfare   95

Chapter 11
    Kingdom Intercessor Unites with the
    Lord of Host for Victory   105

Chapter 12
    Intercessors Called to Overcome Ancient
    Demonic Forces 119

Books by Pernell H. Hewing   136

PART I

Calling forth Intercessors to Prepare...

...FOR THE MINISTRY OF ...
...KINGDOM INTERCESSION

The call comes...

"...from Jesus Christ, who is the faithful witness, and the first begotten of the dead, and the prince of the kings of the earth. Unto him that loved us, and washed us from our sin in his own blood.

"And hath made us kings and priests unto God and his Father; to him be glory and dominion for ever and ever. Amen."
Revelations 1:5-6

The Body of Christ Awaits the Ministry of

Kingdom Intercessor

Rending the Heavens...
...To open the way for the...

KINGDOM OF HEAVEN TO INVADE THE EARTH

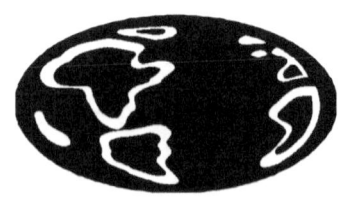

CHAPTER 1

KINGDOM INTERCESSION...

...The Vanguard for the Kingdom of Heaven to Invade the Earth

"The sceptre shall not depart from Judah, nor a lawgiver from between his feet, until Shiloh come; and unto him shall the gathering of the people be." Genesis 49:10

Believers in Jesus Christ and/or Intercessors should not ponder the call to prepare for the ministry of *Kingdom Intercession*. It is the midnight hour of the Church and the Body of Christ; therefore, it is a clarion call for Intercessors to arise and prepare themselves to become *Kingdom Intercessors*. Intercession is a sure movement that has been on the horizon for some time, but now God is orchestrating a new movement which is *"Kingdom Intercession."*

This end-time call to *Kingdom Intercession* is a call for intercessors to prepare for a higher level of intercession. The call is to come forth to become strategists and/or frontline soldiers in the invincible army of the Lord. This is a call to prepare for **Kingdom Intercession** which can be answered by any believer in Jesus Christ. It is, however, a call to intercessors especially to prepare to move to another level of intercession and to get ready to participate in this special end-time move of God.

This **Kingdom Intercession** move of God will thrust Intercession into its higher purpose of opening the way for the Kingdom of Heaven to come on earth as it is in heaven and for the King to invade the Church. Because **Kingdom Intercession** is the Vanguard to open the way for the King to come to His Church, this vanguard is made up of frontline soldiers; that is, ones on the forefront, trailblazers, groundbreakers, pacesetters, etc.

In order to be in the forefront, to be the trailblazer etc; one must be a prepared **Kingdom Intercessor** who has been or is ready to be trained in ground-level intercession, stratospheric intercession, **Priestly** intercession, and now on to **Kingdom Intercession**. The intercessor must be trained strategically and anchored in the Kingdom of Heaven. There is more to this than the call to intercession—It is a call to preparation. It is written...

"*For many are called, but few are chosen.*" Matt. 22:14

One must enter into a covenant with the King of the Kingdom of Heaven to be His **Kingdom Intercessor**.

Kingdom Intercession Opens the Way for The Kingdom of Heaven to Come on Earth

It is the **Kingdom Intercessor** which stands at the forefront of the battle to open the way for the King to return and for the believers/saints to enter into the Kingdom of Heaven. The ministry of **Kingdom Intercession** is the greatest move of God the earth has experienced.

This great move will activate an army of intercessors who are sleeping giants. The devil fears these sold-out, prepared intercessors and tries to keep them under his foot. When these intercessors arise as **Kingdom Intercessors**, they will be the key to opening the way for the King to return and for believers to enter into the Kingdom of Heaven.

Although **Kingdom Intercession** *is* the Vanguard for the Kingdom of Heaven to invade the earth, **Kingdom Intercessors** must covenant with the Lord for their position as a **Kingdom Intercessor**. One's covenant position with the King to be His **Kingdom Intercessor** does not come by the new birth alone, nor by a sincere desire. It comes through covenant-making with the King for the assignment as **Kingdom Intercessor**. Covenant making has always been God's way and will be His way to bring forth His end-time **Kingdom Intercessor**.

God does everything by Covenant--A study of scripture reveals that all of God's actions are based on Covenant. One enters a covenant agreement with God when he/she enters the Body of Christ. Although that one has been 'called out' of the world into the Body of Christ, he/she must covenant with God to enter into *Kingdom Intercession* and to become a *Kingdom Intercessor* unto the Lord and for the Lord.

Many intercessors believe they have done all necessary to be intercessors of the Lord, and that they are ready for every level of intercession. However, *Kingdom Intercession* requires a covenant because a covenant for *Kingdom Intercession* is a covenant for a death-walk into intercession for the King. The covenant to become a *Kingdom Intercessor* unto the King of kings and be the Vanguard standing in the forefront of the battle front is a higher level prayer and higher level of covenant.

"And take the helmet of salvation, and the sword of the Spirit, which is the word of God:

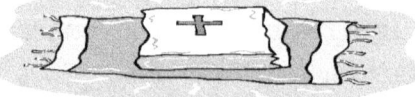

"Praying always with all prayer and supplication in the Spirit, and watching thereunto with all perseverance and supplication for all saints." Ephesians 6:17-18

IDENTIFYING REALMS OF *ANOINTING* FOR PRAYER AND INTERCESSION

As one comes to this landmark place in his/her decision to become a *Kingdom Intercessor*, it becomes necessary to identify positioning in the call to intercession. There are four spiritual realms of prayer and intercession with the accompanying *anointing* for answers to prayer and for ministry.

Every born-again believer in Jesus Christ, therefore, needs to understand these four spiritual realms in order to know where he/she is in position for the authority for answers to prayer and to minister in these levels. The Prayer *Anointings* and the power for them are held out by God to every believer/saint so that one can be delegated authority for answers to prayer in a particular realm:

The four spiritual realms of prayer/intercession anointing

- *The Prayer of Power – Believer's Prayer – Ground-Level Prayer*

- *Warfare Prayer Anointing— Prayer Warrior Stratospheric Prayer*

- *The Priestly Prayer Anointing -- Prayer for People*

- *The Kingly Prayer Anointing – Kingdom Intercession for Kingdom purposes*

One receives *anointing* and authority in a realm of the Spirit for answers to prayer as one enters into the fullness of the requirements for that level. The believer/intercessor is given *anointing* and authority for answers to prayer for a particular realm of the spirit and then given the SPIRITUAL AUTHORITY to walk in power and authority for the ministry of prayer for that spiritual realm.

The *anointing* and power for prayer in a particular realm of the Spirit opens the way for the one praying to receive answers to prayer at that realm. It is important for the believer to know where his/her authority lies and also where the one praying with and for him/her has *anointing* and authority. Also, the intercessor needs to know the need to move to another realm and how to move to the next realm for prayer.

> *"Death to self is the key to walking in any one of the Anointings of prayer in a particular spiritual realm..."*

The *anointing* for authority for answers to prayer in a particular spiritual realm can be walked in simultaneously, but the believer may have the *anointing* and authority for answer to prayer in only one realm of the spirt if he/she has not paid the price for more than one realm of the spirit. However, all four spiritual realm are open to the believer/saint.

The *anointing* to pray and the authority and power delegated by God to pray in that *anointing* comes from God when the prayer/intercessor has fulfilled God's requirement for that realm of prayer. Since authority in prayer and *ANOINTING* are inextricably interwoven, the *anointing* comes with the delegation of authority by God to pray under a particular *anointing*.

God will not release prayer power nor delegate authority to a rebel, nor to one who has a history of rebellion. One will, therefore, need to have revisited all church, family life, and all places where one rebelled against delegated authority; and allow God to cleanse him/her of the sin of rebellion at all points. Just as one cannot cast out a demon if one carries the same spirit, one cannot pray in a certain area if that one has not been released from his/her own sin or rebellion in a particular area.

Anointing for answers to prayer in a particular spiritual realm is sacred, and the fullness of that *anointing* and the power of that *anointing* for answers to prayer is given to the believer whose life is submitted to God. For God to delegate authority in prayer to a believer, he/she must be in the position with God that God can tell that believer what to do, and he/she will do it. Then God will do what He needs to do to minister His power in that situation. One cannot come into that close position with God with any hint of rebellion in him/her.

For a believer to earn the position with God so that God will delegate the authority to him/her, the believer needs to have a history of submission and obedience to God for all God has revealed to him/her at that level. Death to self is the key to walking in any one of the prayer *Anointings*.

Until a believer has paid the price of death to self that is needed for a particular *anointing*, that *anointing* nor the prayer power and the power to stand in that position before God and receive an answer will not be bestowed by God. The believer/saint must always be faithful in one's prayer *anointing* if he/she is to receive the next *anointing in prayer*.

Practical Exercises

***Kingdom Intercession** is not an insignificant call. It is not a call one chooses because one wants to answer the call to the ministry. It is a call of the King of kings and Lord of lords. If one is reading this and his/her heart is saying yes, this call is for me, it means that the King has brought that one to a position of testing and trial because the King believes that He can trust that one.*

*There is still a mile of time to go before one can enter the covenanted position of **Kingdom Intercessor**. To begin this trek towards becoming a **Kingdom Intercessor**, one must enter into a covenant with the Lord for this higher level of intercession. Before making that covenant for **Kingdom Intercession**, reread the preceding chapter with care as follows.*

Read the preface several times

After reading the preface, read chapter one as follows:

Read a paragraph, Meditate on the paragraph, Pray the paragraph for yourself. Spend much time with this chapter.

If you say yes to the call and believe that you are ready for this call, complete the covenant agreement which follows.

COVENANT AGREEMENT

FOR PREPARATION FOR *KINGDOM INTERCESSOR*

Dear Lord. . .

*Teach me your way to pray. I need to be taught how to pray by you to prepare to become your **Kingdom Intercessor**.*

*I commit myself to you, Lord, and promise to do what you lead in order to become your **Kingdom Intercessor**. I commit myself to diligent study as you lead and to stay with what you lead until I learn what you set forth for me to read.*

*I commit my time and my resources to learning how to become your **Kingdom Intercessor**. I will be obedient when you show me what I need to do to enter into the full measure of your appointed Kingdom life. Lord, as I sign this covenant agreement, I am agreeing to enter into training with Christ for **Kingdom Intercession**. Thank you, Lord, for accepting me and my commitment.*

Name _____ Ph._____

Address ———————————— Zip _____

City/State_____

Witness _____
Title _____

Practical Exercises

*The call to Kingdom Intercession is no small insignificant call, therefore, it is important to move into this call slowly. For that reason, stop here and sanctify yourself in the truth of **anointing** for answers to prayer and for ministry in a particular spiritual realm for answers to prayer and for ministry for a deeper understanding of and preparation for Kingdom Intercession.*

Obtain and read the book: **"Understanding and Submit-ting to Spiritual Authority brings Power, Authority and Anointing,"** by Dr. Pernell H. Hewing, (Sanctuary Word Press, 921 West Main Street, Whitewater, WI.

> *Read and study this book, "Understanding Spiritual Authority...." Take as long as necessary to understand the four spiritual realms for anointing and authority delegated by God for ministry. You don't have to complete the Practical Exercises unless you desire*

Chapter 2

The Special *Anointing* and Power of the Believer's Prayer

The *Anointing* of Power and Authority

The first of the four special realms of spiritual authority of prayer one enters into for power in prayer is the Believer's Prayer. This is prayer which grows out of the believers walk with God, and as that one becomes established in the Lord, he/she begins and grows in ground level praying. This prayer may not be prayer of power in the onset of the believer's walk with God, but will become powerful as the believer grows and becomes more established in his/her salvation.

Since prayer of power is the foundation of the spiritual life and living for the Lord, it is important that this level is solidly built because it is a foundation for all of one's prayer life. Often believers begin praying for any and everything without the power, without the *anointing* for answer to much of that for which they pray. This type of praying defies receiving strategic answers to prayer.

Perhaps many praying and ministering without the *anointing* don't know that they need the *anointing* and authority to receive answers in a particular level, or they don't know that they don't have the power and authority for answers to most of which they pray. Perhaps they have not seen it nor expected to have power and authority in prayer, and the Lord may or may not answer some of the prayers.

All of the spiritual life is built upon prayer and lived out by prayer. Therefore, one needs to know that the authority is what causes God to answer prayer. Praying without the *anointing* shows a lack of respect for God, as it is a lack of respect for the power of God just as ministering or moving in a spiritual realm without the *anointing* and power of God is moving under one's own power.

Rejecting God and His power is an assault to God. That one praying then becomes God in him/herself and is in rebellion against God. The *anointing* of POWER and authority in prayer is the first and foremost *anointing* needed. Other *Anointings* are needed for power for fuel.

> *Rejecting God and His power is an assault to God.*

The Believer's PRAYER OF POWER is the first and foremost prayer in which one becomes established. Prayer of power includes prayer for Christian Living devotional prayer, prayer of confession,  prayer for things and people. Although this may be considered training ground prayer, it can have great power and the need is great to complete this level of praying before moving to the next realm

A deep understand of the work of the Spirit and the blood working together is basic to completing the requirement for *anointing* of power in this realm. The *Kingdom Intercessor* must spend time here to establish him/herself in a sure knowledge of the power in the blood of

Jesus. This requires waiting quietly and patiently before the Lord in childlike, persevering, and expectant faith with a soul opened to a powerful experience of the wonderful power of the blood of Jesus. One must meet the requirements and move into position with God which He holds out to that one in order for that one to have the *anointing* of power for answer to prayer at this realm or any one of the other realms. All the other *realms of prayer* will need the PRAYER OF POWER for fuel. The *prayer* of power will serve as the steam which powers a steam engine to move one to power in prayer.

The other Prayer *Anointings* are as the steam engine going forth with great power fueled by the Believer's *prayer* and *anointing* Power of the Holy Ghost. As one fulfills the requirement for the *prayer* of Power, that one's prayer brings the fullness of Christ into operation by the blood of Jesus and the Holy Spirit working for and in the believer for answered prayer. Realm One, ground-level prayer can become that prayer of power that allows the believer's life for God, to do the works of the Risen Savior, and to and receive answers. There is warfare prayer in ground-level praying, but that is to battle the forces on the ground level. For practical purposes attention will be given about another level of warfare in the Realm Two which follows.

REALM 2: WARFARE PRAYER *ANOINTING* — *PRAYER WARRIOR* – STRATOSPHERIC PRAYER

The *Prayer Warrior* battles in warfare and the power of darkness against satan's control. This realm is of special interest to satan, and satan will do everything in his power to side-track, hinder, weaken, and destroy the *Prayer Warrior* and the *Prayer Warrior's anointing* at this point.

Satan fights to keep God's ways and God's desires out of the Church and plant his own, and it is the *Prayer Warrior*s satan wants to stop because it is here that satan controls everything. The *Prayer Warrior's anointing* carries the *Prayer Warrior* into satan's territory, but the *Prayer Warrior* has gained his/her *anointing* and authority for completing Realm One. The *Prayer Warrior* gained *anointing* for answered prayer in Realm One. Now the victory for the believer is in his/her *anointing* and authority for this level.

The *Prayer Warrior* may get some battle scars as he/she becomes anchored on this level, but his authority and power is secured by having completed Realm One. The trained *Prayer Warrior* from ground level prayer is now ready to declare war against wickedness and unrighteousness.

The *Prayer Warrior* knows that the battle is fierce because the *Prayer Warrior* comes to the Lord bound by sin and self, both of which must be defeated before the warrior can belong to God fully. It is here the *Prayer Warrior* must fight to the death of self. This fight may be against sexual sin, doubt, anxiety, anger, hatred, unforgiveness, etc.

The *Prayer Warrior* may have thought the battle for self was completed in realm one, but the battle against the self includes selfishness, self-sufficiency, self-control, self-will, self-conceit, independence, self-reliance, etc.

The beginning battle on this realm is to tear down the kingdom self has built. This is the kingdom of self from which man operated before coming into the Kingdom of God fully, and there are forces in the realm where satan is that fights the *Prayer Warrior*—These forces must be defeated before the *Prayer Warrior* can defeat satan.

The *Prayer Warrior* knows that he/she must ...

> "Submit ... therefore to God. Resist the devil, and he will flee from you.
>
> "Draw nigh to God, and he will draw nigh to you. Cleanse your hands, ye sinners; and purify your hearts, ye double minded.
>
> "Be afflicted, and mourn, and weep: let your laughter be turned to mourning, and your joy to heaviness.
>
> "Humble yourselves in the sight of the Lord, and he shall lift you up." James 4:7-10

Another battle of warfare the *Prayer Warrior* must fight is the battle between Jesus, the Holy Spirit, and the Word of God. This fight is against satan, against wickedness, and against evil spirits. The *Prayer Warrior* has been given the gift of authoritative prayer while walking in full obedience to all the revealed will of God received on Realm One.

When the *Prayer Warrior* comes out against satan, he/she knows that authoritative prayer is not doing anything in his/her own strength, but doing it via the throne. That one learned on Realm One that authoritative prayer is not begging God against His will; it is notifying God of what He knows must be done. The *Prayer Warrior* will win because of having fulfilled the requirement for Realm One.

The battle is fierce for the *Prayer Warrior*, but the *Prayer Warrior* learns in the heat of the battle that in order to receive the *anointing* of power in prayer in spiritual warfare, one must fight to the death of self and all that satan controls. The *Prayer Warrior* fights until the victory has been won in order to receive the *anointing* and authority for victory on this realm of the Spirit.

The *Prayer Warrior* must fight until he/she knows that Satan is defeated, the battle has been won, and Jesus Christ,is Lord. The *Prayer Warrior* then is called to keep the victory. The weapons the *Prayer Warrior* has been given authority and *anointing* to use to fight in this Realm are...

- ♦ Salvation   ♦ Righteousness
- ♦ The Gospel of Peace ♦ The Name of the Lord Jesus
- ♦ The Word of God

With these weapons the *Prayer Warrior* is positioned to fight the battle for spiritual control to victory. The Lord has deeply implanted in the heart of the *Prayer Warrior* the following truth:

"... *I am Alpha and Omega, first and the last: ...*" Rev. 1:11

The lesson the *Prayer Warrior* learns in this realm is that **"The battle is not his/hers, but the Lord's."**

It is written...

"Therefore I say unto you, What things soever ye desire, when ye pray, believe that ye receive them, and ye shall have them." Mark 11:24

With authoritative prayer, the **Prayer Warrior** can command whatever hinders to stop, can bind evil spirits, can loose Holy Spirits, can halt activities of satan, *all in the name of the Lord Jesus.* The **Prayer Warrior**'s ministry of intercession brings power in authoritative prayer which is used in spiritual warfare against satan. Again, this authority is given to the **Prayer Warrior** because of his/her position of authority obtained in Realm One. It is written ...

"Behold, I give unto you power to tread on serpents and scorpions, and over all the power of the enemy: and nothing shall by any means hurt you." Luke 10:19

"And these signs shall follow them that believe; In my name shall they cast out devils; they shall speak with new tongues." Mark 16:17

Practical Exercises

*Since **Kingdom Intercession** is orchestrated by God, and some have not understood and/or have not completed the requirements for the various REALMS, it becomes necessary to prepare well.*

For the one serious about preparation for Kingdom Intercession, pause here and spend some time reading and praying through the following book:

"The Ministry of the Mizpeh Covenant,"
By Dr. Pernell H. Hewing,
(Sanctuary Word Press.

Information is available in book list.

CHAPTER 3

THE HIGHER REALMS OF PRAYER POWER

Realm 2: Prophetic Prayer *Anointing*

The higher purpose the *Prayer Warrior* learns from the Lord in REALM TWO is the power in prophetic prayer and intercession. The **Prophetic Anointing** is important to the *Prayer Warrior's* *anointing* of power to speak the Word of God in Power in prayer against satan to satan, and to created an atmosphere for answers to prayer. The *Prayer Warrior* begins to learn that *Prayer Warrior*s can be the mouth of God in prayer as well as in prophesying to people and for people.

The **Prophetic Anointing in prayer** includes the three spiritual gifts to speak which are *prophecy*, the *gifts of tongues*, and *interpretation of tongues*. All of these can produce answers in prayer. Prophecy is speaking God's word and those words can be spoken to create answers to prayer. To prophesy or to speak God's Word, the believer needs the *anointing* of power from REALM ONE.

The prophetic words spoken in prayer and intercession by God's *prophetic intercessor* are words God put in the mouth of that one. These prophetic words, whether prayed for people or spoken against the devil, will have the anointed power for that prophetic word to work the works of God in power and in answer to prayer.

The *Prayer Warrior's anointing* for power against satan cannot come forth with power unless the believer has the underlying *anointing* of power which was made available to him/her in Realm One. In order for God to delegate authority in prayer for the believer/saint against satan in this realm where the prophetic *anointing* is needed, the believer/saint has to have died to self on Realm One and in Realm Two.

The pure prophetic *anointing* in prayer is badly needed for the *Prayer Warrior* because words have great power and the prophetic *anointing* is in the tongue and can be used in prayer. The Prophetic Word can speak life or death. That is why the *Prayer Warrior*, must die to self in each Spiritual Realm and have his/her being in Christ.

Realm 3: The *Priestly* Prayer *Anointing*

The *Priestly Anointing* in prayer is that special *anointing* where the believer is delegated authority to represent man to God and God to man. The *Priestly Anointing* in prayer includes three spiritual gifts, which are *Wisdom, Knowledge,* and *Discerning of Spirits*. The believer/saint as priest intercedes for the people.

The believer as priest is trusted with God's secret, the revelation gifts. As the believer/saint takes his/her position as priest, he/she will know when danger is near and will offer the people God's mercy. The believer as priest stands between God and the people and makes intercession for them. The believer as priest is willing to take the place of the one or ones for which that priest intercedes and will hold back God's judgment.

Because of the power with God and for God, the believer needs to have paid the price in death to self and in perfect submission to the perfect will of God as he/she stands before God as a priest for others. That one should have a history of perfect obedience to God to be anointed for power in this realm of the Spirit. That is why it was necessary to have repented of all rebellion and disobedience to authority before coming to be delegated authority for answer to prayer for the people.

The believer/saint with the *Priestly Anointing* in prayer must have passed through the realm of the Spirit where one has the *Anointing* of Power in prayer, and the *Prayer Warrior*s warfare and **prophetic** *anointing*. Often all three of these *Anointings* will come to bear in the *Priestly Anointing* if the believer is delegated authority to receive answer to prayer in all three of these realms of the Spirit. A believer can receive this triple *anointing* of power in these realms if one has been submissive to God in every way he/she knows up to this point.

The *Priestly Anointing* in prayer is most sacred just as every *anointing* of the Lord which God holds out to a believer. This most sacred *anointing* is held out to whomever is willing to pay the price of death to self through submission to God and obedience to all He has revealed to that one. This is what brings power and authority for prayers to be answered in any realm. Any believer/saint, therefore, who is willing to pay the price and make the sacrifice can have this *Priestly Anointing* of Power in prayer.

Realm 4: The *Kingly Prayer Anointing*

The KINGLY ANOINTING is the *anointing* for *Kingdom Intercessor*. It is an *anointing* of great power in prayer. A King is one with the power of a ruler. **The Kingly Anointing** in prayer is held out to that one who has paid the price in submission to God and obedience to all that God has revealed. God now wants to delegate His true power, His power of rulership to that one if he/she is willing to pay the price for this great *anointing*. The **Kingly Anointing** gives power and is an *anointing* of supreme power. It is written...

> "For the kingdom of God is not meat and drink; but righteousness, and peace, and joy in the Holy Ghost.
>
> "For he that in these things serveth Christ is acceptable to God, and approved of men." Romans 14:17-18

Where there is a kingdom, there is a king, and there are principles of the kingdom. The *Kingdom Intercessor* must earn the authority for answers to prayer in this realm by having completed requirements for authority in prayer in the previous realms. Along with authority for prayer, God also gives authority to rule and reign in kingdom work and to receive answers to prayer for this realm.

One must receive **Kingly *Anointing*** for power in prayer, and that one is then given **Kingly Authority** for *Kingdom Intercession*. The *Kingdom Intercession Anointing* gives power and authority for answered prayer to rule and be a ruler in the King's business. The *Kingdom Intercessor Anointing* gives the intercessor the faith of God who is the sovereign ruler.

The King wants to delegate His Kingly Authority in prayer to the intercessor along with the authority to minister as king in kingdom work. This one, however, must be prepared for and living in the Kingdom. With the delegation of authority in *Kingdom Intercession* comes the Kingly *Anointing* in prayer and intercession. The believer still needs the **Prayer Warrior's Prophetic *Anointing*** and *Priestly Anointing* in prayer to experience the **Kingly *Anointing*** for *Kingdom Intercession*. The different *anointing* work when they are needed only as the believer is led by the Holy Spirit.

The *Kingdom Intercession* **Kingly** *Anointing* demands obedience. Believers who are obedient to God are connected to God's will. They have moved from being connected for the will of the ministry and are now connected only to God's will. That one now knows that everything else is subject to change. Before the believer/saint can and will do the will of God, he/she must first be subject to God's authority. When obedience is complete, a believer can meet requirements for the ***Kingly Prayer Anointing***.

Practical Exercises

> ***Time to pause*** *again to anchor self in the sacred **anointing** for power and answers to prayer. Read, Pray, and study the book:*
>
> **"Shiloh El-Beth-el, Calling Believers in Christ in Preparation for the Ministry of the Kingdom of Heaven."**
> *By Dr. Pernell H. Hewing,*
>
> *Reading and studying the information presented in this book is critical to understanding the call to the Kingdom of Heaven and how to prepare for the Kingly **anointing**. Completing Practical Exercises optional.*

PART II

PREPARATION OF THE INTERCESSOR

ADORNING OF THE INTERCESSOR

SANCTIFICATION OF THE INTERCESSOR

FOR KINGDOM INTERCESSION

Put on therefore, as the elect of God, holy and beloved, bowels of mercies, kindness, humbleness of mind, meekness, longsuffering;" Colossians 3:12

THE INTERCESSOR IS CALLED TO THE KING'S CHAMBER

The Intercessor must undergo intense preparation by the King. Healing and deliverance are complete before one reaches this place of being called for this important position.

The special requirements now are cleansing, consecration, and sanctification.

Sanctification is separation. The intercessor now must be ready to be taken out of his/her surroundings by the King's commandment and set aside or separated as His possession and for His service. The Intercessor is then counted holy unto the King, and prepared for Kingdom living and Kingdom Service.

Chapter 4

Preparation for the Ministry of *Kingdom Intercession*

The call today is loud and clear, and there is a clear echo behind that call of the Lord which says ... *"Come to the Ministry of Kingdom Ministry."* This call is issued to the Church, to the body of Christ, and to every born-again believer in the Lord Jesus Christ which makes up the Church and the Body of Christ. However, the intercessor must prepare him/herself for this rich experience of *Kingdom Intercession*, for the new relationship with the King as His intercessor.

The Intercessor's **Kingdom** Ministry is a ministry of love and a ministry of praise and adoration. This is a ministry that leads to absolute surrender, a ministry that leads to an intimate relationship with a loving savior and a Priest/King. Many in the Body of Christ have a deep cry that is of one sick with love for the Lord, but that one cannot seem to touch Him. Their heart is saying...

> *"I charge you, O daughters of Jerusalem, if ye find my beloved, that ye tell him, that I am sick of love."* Song of Solomon 5:8

The Intercessor's **Kingdom** Ministry, the ministry of the *Kingdom Intercession* is perhaps that for which one's heart longs. It is a ministry whose builder and maker is God. It is a city for which Abraham looked. It is written...

> *"For he looked for a city which hath foundations, whose builder and maker is God."* Hebrews 11:10

The Intercessor's Kingdom Ministry call has brought many in the Body of Christ to the place in their walk with the Lord where the pull upon their heart daily is for more of the Lord–the place where love for the King abounds. That one then is looking for the Intercessor's ***Kingdom Intercession*** Ministry, which will bring him/her to a place of dwelling with Christ, the place of love, peace, and joy with the Savior. That one is looking for entrance into the Intercessor's ***Kingdom Intercession*** Ministry.

The heart for The Intercessor's **Kingdom** Ministry is based on a love relationship of the Lord Jesus. The heart that seeks the Intercessor's **Kingdom** Ministry is the heart which is ready for the Jesus to have full possession and will say…

> *"I am my beloved's, and his desire is toward me."*
> Song of Solomon 7:10

THE INTERCESSOR'S KINGDOM MINISTRY IS A MINISTRY PREPARED BY GOD

The Intercessor's ***Kingdom Intercession*** ministry, the bridal relationship ministry, is prepared by God because the seeking soul has given up every earthly pursuit and is seeking God alone, therefore, following the witness of old…

> *"But now they desire a better country, that is, an heavenly: wherefore God is not ashamed to be called their God: for he hath prepared for them a city."*
> Hebrews 11:16

The call to the ***Kingdom Intercession*** ministry comes to a soul prepared by God and embellished with love. Hear what is said of that soul.

It is written...

> "*Thou art beautiful, O my love, as Tirzah, comely as Jerusalem, terrible as an army with banners.*" Song of Solomon 6:4

This is the state the hungry soul seeks. This heart cries for that promise. What is this Intercessor's ***Kingdom Intercession*** ministry? The intercessor's **Kingdom** ministry is the ministry in the call to a heart of a soul longing to enter into the city of the Living God and into an intimate relationship with the King. It is here that the intercessor touches the heart of God for intercession. It is here that the heart has turned completely to desiring a loving savior to come take up residence in a heart which is hungry for a deep love of the King.

A soul that has come into the Intercessor's **Kingdom** Ministry has come to the living God, and is ready for the ***anointing*** for service. The Called intercessor who has turned away from all others, has set his/her beloved as a seal upon the heart of the King. It is written...

> "*Set me as a seal upon thine heart, as a seal upon thine arm: for love is strong as death; jealousy is cruel as the grave: the coals thereof are coals of fire, which hath a most vehement flame.*" Song of Solomon 8:6

The soul that seeks to come to the Intercessor's **Kingdom** Ministry wants now to come to King Jesus as his intercessor. It is written...

> "*By him therefore let us offer the sacrifice of praise to God continually, that is, the fruit of our lips giving thanks to his name.*" Hebrews 13:15

THE CALL TO *KINGDOM INTERCESSION* IS A CALL TO HOLINESS

The call to the **Kingdom** Ministry of intercession is the call to a ministry of Holiness. It is a call to a new beginning of a Kingdom walk of holiness. As one prepares for this new beginning, that one needs to know that he/she cannot discover this wonderful, long sought-after experience without the supernatural help of the one whose love is sought; that is, the  King of the Kingdom. The King of the Kingdom, who knows that His beloved wants this experience, looks on the intercessor's longing heart and draws that one to Himself.

As one comes to this special ministry of *Kingdom Intercession*, one must be ready to live a life of complete surrender. This will mean holiness, true holiness without any compromise. As it is written, the intercessor's **Kingdom** Ministry is the sum total of one's spiritual life and walk. This Ministry of *Kingdom Intercession* brings together one's Spiritual life and walk and is the sum total of one's experiences with the Lord.

The Call to the *Intercessor's Kingdom Ministry is the call to a death walk.* The depths of the **Kingdom** Ministry **of intercession** one cannot comprehend completely with the natural mind, but be assured that as one enters into the study of *Kingdom Intercession*, the Lord will, by his Spirit, bring that one into the fruition of it. That one will come forth with the heart of the King and all the power of heaven with him/her.

A true death experience brings the Intercessor to the place where the King is that one's life, and without Him there is no life. When that one could not touch Jesus, the heart cried out ...

> *"I opened to my beloved; but my beloved had withdrawn himself, and was gone: my soul failed when he spake: I sought him, but I could not find him; I called him, but he gave me no answer."* Song of Solomon 5:6

Now all is lost until the beloved answers. The Intercessor is crying for the King to reveal His heart, and is longing for the Word the King wants to give.

The Bridegroom is a Holy God and A Holy Bride Must be Concerned with

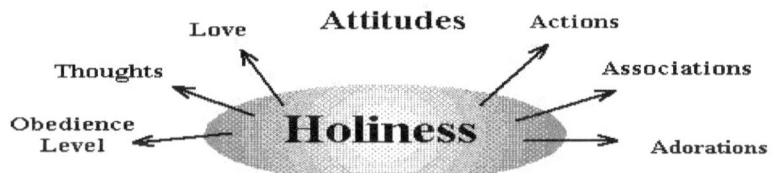

Love Attitudes Actions
Thoughts **Holiness** Associations
Obedience Level Adorations

Holiness must be the governing principle in every area of the bride's life. It must be displayed inwardly and outwardly towards God, oneself, and others.

The Bridegroom Calls the Bride to. . . Be Ye Holy--as God and Jesus are Holy

Holiness is:
  The Displacement of the old man from the Control Center

  Pulling him out of the Driver's Seat

Putting on the New Man--
  the New Holy
  Nature of the Bridegroom -- Jesus Christ

DOORWAY TO *KINGDOM INTERCESSION* AND THE INTERCESSOR'S KINGDOM WALK AND WORK

The Lord now wants to bring the Intercessor into the intimate relationship, the place of new beginnings. This is the beginning of holy love between King Jesus and the ***Kingdom Intercessor***. Just as the intercessor begins life anew, the new beginning is the beginning of a new life—Kingdom Life-- with the King of the Kingdom in the Kingdom.

In the Intercessor's Kingdom Ministry, the intercessor enters into covenant to begin a new walk and work for God in His kingdom which cannot be moved—that place where Jesus Christ is the mediator of the new covenant. It is here the King will bring His intercessor into union with Him.

This new walk and work is entered into because of love and love alone, and the King says to the Intercessor…

> *"Come, my beloved, let us go forth into the field; let us lodge in the villages."*

> *"Let us get up early to the vineyards; let us see if the vine flourish, whether the tender grape appear, and the pomegranates bud forth: there will I give thee my loves."*
> Song of Solomon 7:11-12

In this Intercessor's **Kingdom** Ministry, the Lord ushers His intercessor, the blessed one, into a new world, a world sometimes which that one may not understand. This is a world where the ***Kingdom Intercessor*** will be separated unto Jesus Christ--it is the hidden life with the King. It is a call to a love relationship with Jesus Christ where the cry is…

> *"I am my beloved's and his desire is toward me."*
> Song of Solomon 7:10

A Look at The Intercessor's Kingdom Ministry of Holiness

The Intercessor's **Kingdom** Ministry is not only a ministry of new beginnings, but also a ministry of holiness where the one who accepts this ministry must be holy. It is also a place of overcoming that which should now cease in a life which is tightly woven to God by covenant. The beloved Intercessor's will then hear the King say...

> *"Thou art all fair, my love; there is no spot in thee."*
> Song of Solomon 4:7

In the new intercessor's Kingdom Ministry, the Lord may ratify--that is, confirm or sanction formally--covenants previously entered into with Him. It is time now to enter into another covenant--a covenant to proceed toward a strange country looking...

> *"...for a city which hath foundations, whose builder and maker is God."* Hebrews 11:10

This is a city of love built by love and maintained by love--a love for the King of the Kingdom. It is written...

> *"Many waters cannot quench love, neither can the floods drown it: if a man would give all the substance of his house for love, it would utterly be contemned."* Song of Solomon 8:7

The intercessor's Kingdom Ministry is a ministry of resurrection. The King kisses His beloved with His love and gently chides His chosen one to awake. The Lord, the King of the Kingdom, calls His Intercessor to come alive. He calls tenderly and says...

> *"Awake, awake; put on thy strength, O Zion; put on thy beautiful garments, O Jerusalem, the holy city: for henceforth there shall no more come into thee the uncircumcised and the unclean."* Isaiah 52:1

The call to the **Kingdom Intercessor** is to come into his/her new strength. The intercessor is promised strength, a strength which may increase instead of diminishing because of the Oil of the Holy Spirit which dwells within. This strength is not only physical strength, but also spiritual and mental strength—whatever the need, the supply will be there and the strength will be there for it.

CHAPTER 5

THE INTERCESSOR IS ADORNED WITH KINGDOM GARMENTS

In the Intercessor's **Kingdom** Ministry, the King calls the Intercessor to surrender all, to enter into a deeper depth with Him. The call is personal, but one must hear the call of the Spirit. The challenge for the Intercessor is to move toward a ministry which he/she knows not--this ministry is a place of resurrection--This is a Kingdom love call.

When the full giving of the intercessor reaches the throne and is laid on the altar and left there for the King of the Kingdom to use and deal with as He sees fit, then the intercessor's blessings will flow like a mighty torrent. In addition, the emptiness will leave and a deep satisfaction will take its place. That longing for an earthly companion will no longer be there for the love of the King of the Kingdom will consume away every other desire.

This new beginning of this Intercessor's **Kingdom** Ministry and this new intimate relationship has interwoven into it new strength. It has beautiful garments, garments of prayer, praise, worship, and Oh, so many more spiritual garments. The *King tells* His ***Kingdom Intercessor****, "Awake, put on the new garments."* This is adorning of the Intercessor.

As the intercessor moves into his/her Kingdom position, that one moves into a place of resurrection. That one is brought to a position in the Spirit where it may appear sometimes as though he/she is walking over a hill and can see only sky and ground. Suddenly the King will come into view, thus becoming more real to the intercessors, as he/she becomes more "sold-out" --more hidden in Him.

The Intercessor Called into a Kingdom Position

The King of the Kingdom calls the intercessor into a **Kingdom** position. It is a call to be His alone--to be "sold-out" to Him. As the intercessor becomes "sold out" to Him, he/she becomes hidden in Him. The intercessor will then learn how to walk by faith and not by sight. What he/she, the "sold-out, hidden one," must do now is move out in faith, accepting the King's promise.

The promise to the intercessor is that the King will do that which is best for His beloved. The King of the Kingdom is a loving King and will bless His *Kingdom Intercessor*. However, the King of the Kingdom will do whatever is necessary to bring His bride to the point where it is the King he/she wants more than the blessings. Know, however, that the King of the Kingdom will not forsake His bride nor leave His bride alone while His bride is moving into that place of complete abandonment.

When the full giving of the intercessor reaches the throne and is laid on the altar and left there for the King of the Kingdom to use and deal with as He sees fit, then the intercessor's blessings will flow like a mighty torrent. In addition, the emptiness will leave and a deep satisfaction will take its place. That longing for an earthly companion will no longer be there for the love of the King of the Kingdom will consume away every other desire.

Although the intercessor cannot give all in his/her own strength, the Spirit of the King will lead and guide him/her. The King of the Kingdom will perfect the intercessor's giving of self as He desires; and the King of the Kingdom, Jesus Christ, will perfect that one's consecration. He will perfect that which concerns His *Kingdom Intercessor* and the chosen one can trust in these words...

> *"The LORD will perfect that which concerneth me: thy mercy, O LORD, endureth for ever: forsake not the works of thine own hands."* Psalms 138: 8

THE CALL HAS BEEN ANSWERED, THE STRIPPING MUST BEGIN. THE HEART OF THE

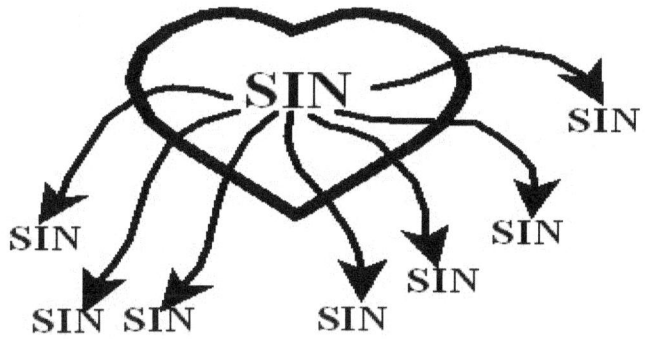

INTERCESSOR'S MUST BE STRIPPED

One coming to the intercessor's **Kingdom** Ministry comes bearing the bruises, the scars, and the wounds of having lived in a sin-sick world. The King of the Kingdom awaits a chaste intercessor, but unlike a human King, He does not wait for the intercessor to prepare him/herself. He stands ready to prepare His bride for that holy union, the perfect intimacy. The King of the Kingdom gives Himself to preparing His intercessor.

It is written…

"That he might sanctify and cleanse ... with the washing of water by the word,

"That he might present ...to himself a glorious church, not having spot, or wrinkle, or any such thing; but that it should be holy and without blemish." Eph. 5:26-27

The prospective **Kingdom Intercessor** comes bearing loneliness and disappointment, having suffered much loss during a lifetime of struggling for survival, striving to find love and acceptance in the world. The disappointments of life have brought sorrow from which has spun self-pity and sometimes depression.

The blessed intercessor who has now been called to the **Kingdom** by the King to become His intercessor comes with a broken heart hidden beneath much pain. Some wounds may be deep and the laceration extensive. The pain is deep, saddening, and throbbing all the time. Some wounds may not be open sores, but hidden so deep inside that the prospective bride may not know they are there. It will mean that one must choose whether he/she is willing to pay the price now in preparation for that coveted position and allow the hidden pain to surface.

PART II PRACTICAL EXERCISES

*The Intercessor's **Kingdom** Ministry is or could be the sum total of your preparation for that final assent into the Holy of Holies to spend your life in the presence of the Lord. IT IS A MINISTRY OF INTIMACY WITH JESUS CHRIST. It will mean that one must choose if he/she is willing to prepare for that coveted position.*

The practical exercise *which will appear at the end of Part II, Part III, Part IV and Part V may appear at first to be just a reading assignment; however, if you follow the slow reading, the meditating, and the praying of the paragraphs as outlined below, your life will be catapulted into a realm of the Spirit which will take you away from the struggle to belong totally to the Lord.*

Part II *introduces you to the **Intercessor's Ministry** in the Body of Christ. Do you want to enter into that ministry? Spend one week with this information, however, it may take weeks, months, or more time.*

DIRECTIONS: *The purpose of this practical exercise is to help you obtain a firm understanding of what the intercessor's **Kingdom** Ministry in the Body of Christ is and help you examine yourself to determine what is needed to be healed, cleansed, and established in your life in order to enter into the Intercessor's **Kingdom** Ministry.*

To complete this exercise, meet with the Lord three to four times a week. Read PART II. Then reread PART II taking one paragraph or more paragraphs at a time. Read slowly. Think on what you read, then pray that for yourself. Do the same with scriptures. Meditate on the scriptures and pray the scriptures.

When you come to illustrations, note the words in the illustration and pray for revelation of what is in that picture which may shed light for you—for healing, for cleansing, for deliverance, etc. When you finish the meeting time, stop, and pray. Then ask the Lord to give you revelations for yourself. Write what you receive.

At the end of the week, review what you wrote and write a brief review of what was revealed to you during the week.

Notes

CHAPTER 6

THE KING COMES TO PREPARE THE INTERCESSOR FOR THE KINGDOM

> *"FOR OTHER FOUNDATION CAN NO MAN LAY THAN THAT IS LAID, WHICH IS JESUS CHRIST." I COR. 3:11*

Jesus Christ must come on the scene to prepare the Intercessor for this **Kingdom Intercession**. Jesus Christ, the King is a comforter, healer and deliverer. He is sent to comfort all who mourn and to all who seek Him for comfort. The prospective **Kingdom Intercessor** has turned from seeking comfort and love from the world and now has come to Jesus for that comfort and love.

Jesus comes on the scene to give the prospective **Kingdom Intercessor** consolation which will not only support that one under sorrow, but turn the sorrow into songs of praise. The intercessor needs healing and cleansing on a deeper level. The intercessor comes to the Kingdom with hidden brokeness, and Jesus Christ, the King, comes to heal the brokenhearted. He said in His Word...

"The Spirit of the Lord is upon me, because he hath anointed me to preach the gospel to the poor; he hath sent me to heal the brokenhearted, to preach deliverance to the captives, and recovering of sight to the blind, to set at liberty them that are bruised," Luke 4:18

Jesus Christ, the King, makes Himself available to the one seeking *to become a* **Kingdom Intercessor**. He comes to heal and cleanse; however, the prospective **Kingdom**

Intercessor must see and know his/her sin and confess sin before the King heals and delivers. It is written...

> *"If we confess our sins, he is faithful and just to forgive us our sins, and to cleanse us from all unrighteousness."*
> I John 1:9

The Prospective ***Kingdom Intercessor*** may have been born again for sometime, but his/her salvation may be surface salvation because the heart is full of sin which has spun from the hurts and disappointments of the past. The sin in the hidden heart may include....*jealousy, anger, bitterness, hatred, resentment, dishonesty, unforgiveness, and many others.* These sins must be known, uncovered, acknowledged, confessed, and put away. The King then comes on the scene to forgive the sins and to cleanse the prospective ***Kingdom Intercessor*** from unforgiveness.

THE INTERCESSOR MUST BE STRIPPED OF EXCESS BAGGAGE IN PREPARATION FOR KINGDOM MINISTRY

The prospective ***Kingdom Intercessor*** comes to the King with much excess baggage fostered by unforgiveness. Unfortunately, the Intercessor may not know the truth and needs to know that the truth will make him/her free. The truth of the Intercessor's unforgiveness is buried in the heart as in a vault of hidden treasure. In that vault is a confidential file filled with the names of people and incidents of life that have not been forgiven. Jesus Christ, the King of the Kingdom, has to gently take the intercessor to the vault, open the door, take out the confidential file, and have the intercessor take the names and incidents out one by one to bring forth forgiveness, healing and love.

VAULT of Hidden Treasure

"UNFORGIVENESS"

What the King will do with the confidential file is to bring to remembrance what pain was connected to the unforgiveness. The Intercessor has to first know the hurt and pain, realize the unforgiveness is there, confess the unforgiveness, and ask forgiveness for holding the unforgiveness.

The King will lead the **Kingdom Intercessor** to acknowledge the hurts, and the Intercessor can then allow the King to heal the hurts. *The Intercessor's heart must be stripped and prepared to receive Kingdom love from the King. It is written...*

> "For from within, out of the heart of men, proceed evil thoughts, adulteries, fornications, murders,
>
> "Thefts, covetousness, wickedness, deceit, lasciviousness, an evil eye, blasphemy, pride, foolishness:
>
> "All these evil things come from within, and defile the man." Mark 7:21-23

The prospective **Kingdom Intercessor** comes to the King of the Kingdom with a heart of stone, encased with SELF, self-will, selfishness, self-conceit, self-righteousness, etc. Jesus Christ and His love and His salvation may be buried under many unholy thoughts which may include all or some of the following: envying, vanity, doubt, deceit, suspicion, covetousness, jealousy, lying, sorrow, misery, depression, stubbornness, unforgiveness, resentment, rebellion, hatred, anger, idolatry, and bitterness. The heart needs stripping. It is written...

> *"The heart is deceitful above all things, and desperately wicked: who can know it?"* Jeremiah 17:9

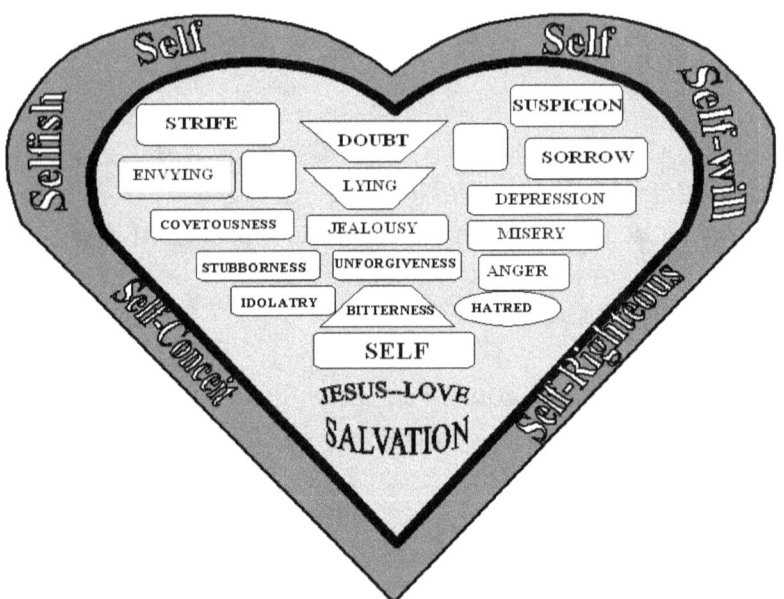

"All these evil things come from within, and defile the man." **Mark 7:23**

The King Receives the *Kingdom Intercessor* as His Bride

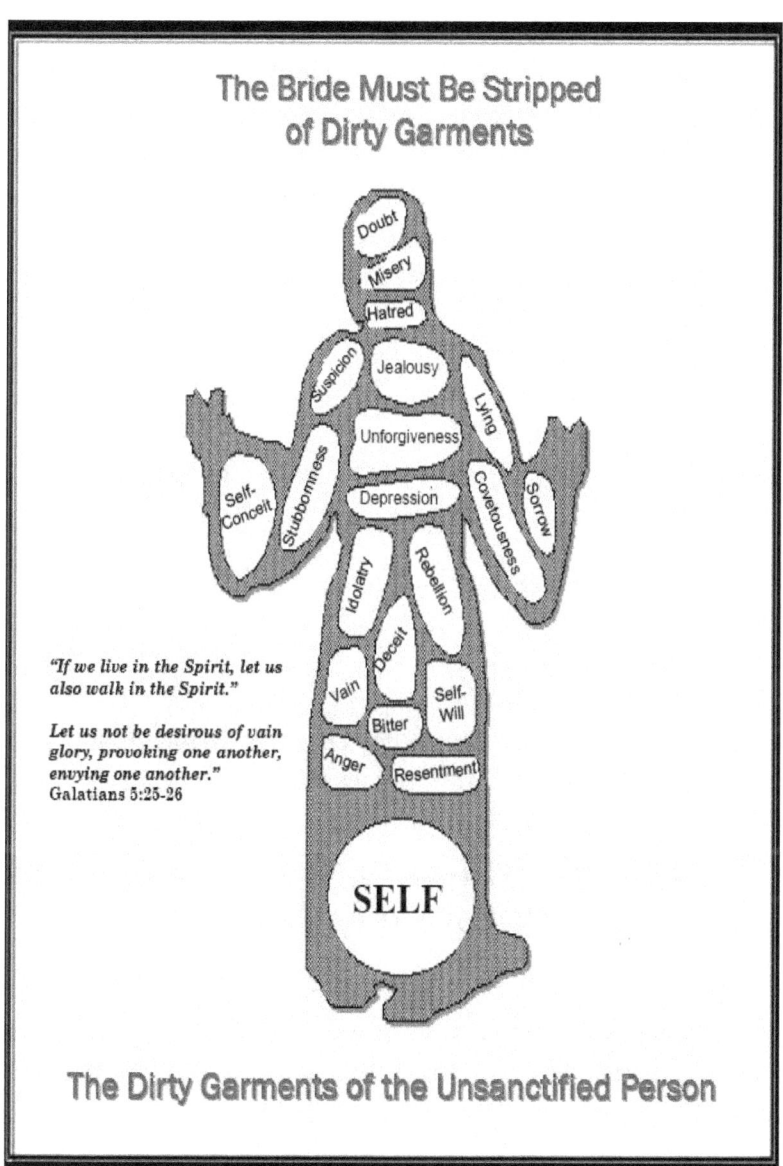

The prospective ***Kingdom Intercessor*** has a sincere desire for the King; however; it takes time for the stripping to be completed. As rapidly as the intercessor allows, the King replaces *selfishness* with His Lordship, *unkindness* with *brotherly kindness, resentment* with *love, unforgiveness* with *forgiveness, harshness* with *gentleness, rebellion* with *submissiveness, pride* with *humility*. This exchange will take place as rapidly as the bride allows. When this is done, the King calls the bride to arise. It is written...

> *"And besides this, giving all diligence, add to your faith virtue; and to virtue knowledge;*
>
> *"And to knowledge temperance; and to temperance patience; and to patience godliness;*
>
> *"And to godliness brotherly kindness; and to brotherly kindness charity.*
>
> *"For if these things be in you, and abound, they make you that ye shall neither be barren nor unfruitful in the knowledge of our Lord Jesus Christ."* II Peter 1:5-8

THE PROSPECTIVE *KINGDOM INTERCESSOR* MUST BE STRIPPED OF DIRTY GARMENTS

The Intercessor's garments are embedded with sin from walking in the flesh and living a carnal life. Now the Intercessor must have his/her ***foot dipped in oil*** for true holiness. The Intercessor must now confess sin, and the King must forgive the sin before the chosen one can come into the fullness of the Holy *Kingdom Relationship*.

It is written...

"If we live in the Spirit, let us also walk in the Spirit.

"Let us not be desirous of vain glory, provoking one another, envying one another." Galatians 5:25-26

Finally the King says to the Intercessor...

"...put off concerning the former conversation the old man, which is corrupt according to the deceitful lusts;

"And be renewed in the spirit of your mind;

"And that ye put on the new man, which after God is created in righteousness and true holiness.

"Wherefore putting away lying, speak every man truth with his neighbour: for we are members one of another.

"Be ye angry, and sin not: let not the sun go down upon your wrath:

"Neither give place to the devil." Ephesians 4:22-27

THE KING COMES TO PUT THE ROBE OF RIGHTEOUSNESS ON THE INTERCESSOR

"Nevertheless the foundation of God standeth sure, having this seal, The Lord knoweth them that are his. And, let every one that nameth the name of Christ depart from iniquity.

"But in a great house there are not only vessels of gold and of silver, but also of wood and of earth; and some to honour, and some to dishonour.

"If a man therefore purge himself from these, he shall be a vessel unto honour, sanctified, and meet for the master's use, and prepared unto every good work."
II Tim. 2:19-21

The King comes to cloth the Intercessor with His robe of righteousness for the Kingdom. Righteousness is whatever God is, whatever God requires, and whatever God commands. When there is some thing in one's relationship to another, there is also something wrong in that one's relationship to God. That is and a violation of God's righteousness. Unrighteousness brings one to act unjustly, to commit evil acts. Unrighteousness also causes one to violate God's law and neglect the true God. This is reflected in one's adherence to the world and to sin.

The intercessor who has worn the garment of unrighteousness has been missing the mark: that is, walking in lawlessness, wickedness, and falling short of righteousness and violating the divine law. The intercessor cannot be unjust, false, and deceitful. Now the King of the Kingdom strips off that robe of unrighteousness and cloths the intercessor with His robe of righteousness.

When the King comes to the intercessor with the oil of joy, He replaces the spirit of mourning with the oil of joy, and makes the face shine because mourning disfigures the face. The King comes to give the intercessor the garment of praise for the spirit of heaviness. The beautiful garment of praise will envelop the Intercessor and the shackles of heaviness will be broken. The King now comes to the Intercessor to give open joy for secret mourning.

THE ADORNING OF THE
KINGDOM INTERCESSOR

The King is a Holy God, and an intercessor must be concerned with holiness--a true holiness which embraces the intercessor's attitudes, actions, associations, obedience, thoughts, love, walk and talk. Holiness must be the governing principle in every area of the *Kingdom Intercessor*'s life. It must be displayed inwardly and outwardly towards God, oneself, and others.

The King calls the *Kingdom Intercessor* to be Holy as God and Jesus are Holy. He lets the *Kingdom Intercessor* know that holiness is the displacement of the old man from the control center; that is, pulling him out of the driver's seat of the *Kingdom Intercessor's* life and putting on the new man...the new holy nature of the King, Jesus Christ.

The *Kingdom Intercessor* is Clothed with the Fruit of the Spirit and is adorned with the fruit of the Spirit as he/she bathes in the presence of the King of the Kingdom and experiences the operation of the Holy Spirit. It is written...

"But the fruit of the Spirit is love, joy, peace, longsuffering, gentleness, goodness, faith,

"Meekness, temperance: against such there is no law.

"And they that are Christ's have crucified the flesh with the affections and lust." Galatians 5:22-24

The **Kingdom Intercessor** is now adorned with the fruit of the Spirit, *love, peace, long suffering, forgiveness, patience, gladness, temperance, virtue, knowledge, gentleness, meekness, Godliness, goodness*. These fruits are resting on a foundation of Jesus Christ. It is written...

"For other foundation can no man lay than that is laid, which is Jesus Christ." I Corinthians 3:11

THE *KINGDOM INTERCESSOR* IS SANCTIFIED AND ADORNED

The **Kingdom Intercessor** is sanctified, that is, set apart for the King and is prepared to walk in the beauty of holiness. As he/she is adorned with the fruits and gifts of the Spirit for Kingdom purposes, he/she walks in the beauty of holiness. The Intercessor has now...

"Put on therefore, as the elect of God, holy and beloved, bowels of mercies, kindness, humbleness of mind, meekness, long-suffering;

"Forbearing one another, and forgiving one another, if any man have a quarrel against any: even as Christ forgave you, so also do ye.

"And above all these things put on charity, which is the bond of perfectness ." Col. 3:12-14

The **Kingdom Intercessor** is standing in the righteousness of the King and has chosen to be Holy as He is holy and is now adorned with the gifts of the spirit. That one is walking in the beauty of holiness. The King now looks upon the intercessor and sees the ***Kingdom Intercessor*** as...

- *...good, godly, considerate, forgiving, kind loving, joyful, peaceful, longsuffering, cheerful, gentle, virtuous, knowledgeable,* and stands on the foundation of *love, faith,* and walking in the humility of Jesus Christ.

PRACTICAL EXERCISES

DIRECTIONS: SPEND FOUR WEEKS WITH THIS EXERCISE.

WEEK 1: REREAD PART lll several times. Make notes of revelations and/or directions from the Lord.

Much of what is written here is fresh revelation from Heaven that includes directions for preparing for a life in the Kingdom, for kingdom ministry, and *Kingdom Intercessor*.

Suggested below are some guidelines for completing this exercise. However, please feel free to follow the Holy Spirit in completing the exercise. If you need more time than what is suggested, continue with the exercise as long as necessary for your entering into the fullness of it.

Week 2: Reread each paragraph, pray the paragraph for yourself. Make notes of personal revelations.

Week 3-4: Review each illustration, pray asking the Lord to reveal anything within the illustration that is in you. Allow the Lord to strip you, heal you, and deliver you. Make notes.

Week 4: Pray through your notes and give special attention to any directions for changes and/or call to obedience. Obey every call to obedience before going on to Part IV.

CHAPTER 7

THE INTERCESSOR, PREPARED AND READY FOR *KINGDOM INTERCESSION*

The call to **Kingdom Intercession** is a call to intercession with a passion. The **Kingdom Intercessor** is always ready and alert to establish God's Kingdom on earth since the **Kingdom Intercessor** has fellowship with the King. This heavenly fellowship gives a taste of God's Kingdom in Heaven and what it will be like in heaven with the King. The King brings the Kingdom of Heaven to earth, and this fellowship with the King through prayer and intercession burns passion in the heart of the intercessor.

Intercession with a passion depicts the *Kingdom Intercessor* who has passion for his/her King. The **Kingdom Intercessor** and the King are one in the spirit. Paul gave a glimpse of the mystery of this relationship. It is written...

> "For this cause shall a man leave his father and mother, and shall be joined unto his wife, and they two shall be one flesh.
>
> "This is a great mystery: but I speak concerning Christ and the church." Ephesians 5:31-32

The call to the *Kingdom Intercessor* is to come forth in intercession with a passion. It is a call to forget everything and everyone, and find delight in the King, Jesus Christ. Only when one loves the King more than anything else will one come to know the King's love. The King does not give His authority and *anointing* to one who gives Him little attention and winks at obedience.

Kingdom Intercession Brings Intimacy

Kingdom Intercession brings the intercessor into the presence of the King to receive from the mouth of the King. It is intercession that is engaged in with a passion as prayer becomes more than the outpouring of one's wishes to the Lord. This intimate relationship brings one to the position of touching the heart of God and praying through, working through, and working out that which touches the heart of God -- that is *Kingdom Intercession*.

> *Kingdom Intercession brings one to touch the heart of the King and pray through what is in His heart.*

The one who now has gained entrance into the position with the King as a *Kingdom Intercessor* is the intercessor whose time is spent before God receiving from the heart of God, that is, God's desires for a sin-sick world -- His desire for others and for things of His heart. God's desires become prayer burdens of the *Kingdom Intercessor*. The *Kingdom Intercessor* then in intercession with a passion -- prays, travails -- and appropriates the promises of God's Word until the answer comes.

The *Kingdom Intercessor* prays down on earth the King's desire. Because of the intimate relationship between the King and the *Kingdom Intercessor*, the answer will surely come because the *Kingdom Intercessor* remains in the presence of the King, the Lord Jesus, until the Lord assures the *Kingdom Intercessor* that the prayer has been heard and answered.

In the presence of the King is where intercession with a passion takes place. As the *Kingdom Intercessor* pours out his/her heart in love, in adoration, in care and concern for the problems of this life, the intercessor has the undivided attention of the King and the ready help of the King. This is a King who owns the earth and all therein. It is written...

"The earth is the LORD's, and the fullness thereof; the world, and they that dwell therein." Psalms 24:1

In intercession the *Kingdom Intercessor* finds fulfillment for life as what the intercessor wants is to please the King and the King wants to satisfy and do all for the *Kingdom Intercessor*. *Kingdom Intercession* then brings them together in that holy union which leaves no room for dissatisfaction or incomplete desires. The *Kingdom Intercessor* is fulfilled and is glad to serve his/her King, and the King responds to the needs of the *Kingdom Intercessor*.

Kingdom Work Flows Out of the Holy of Holies

It is in the Holy of Holies where the King whispers secrets in the ears of the beloved *Kingdom Intercessor*, and he/she learns the secrets of the Kingdom. It is in the Holy of

Holies that the ***Kingdom Intercessor*** pours out of his/her heart the needs and concerns of and for others, and the King responds to the heart cry of his ***Kingdom Intercessor*** -- this is ***Kingdom Intercession***. This is the results of intercession with a passion.

It is in the Holy of Holies where the battle is waged against satan. The King teaches the ***Kingdom Intercessor*** how to fight and the King also stands ready to protect his ***Kingdom Intercessor*** from unseen forces. This is the role of the intercessor to fight for the heritage of the King. This is the ***Kingdom Intercessor*** in intercession, one who is worshipping, praising, and adoring the King, and one who is battling the host of hell for a heavenly King.

To answer the call to ***Kingdom Intercession*** is to answer the call to receive the love of the King, and to come into the Holy of Holies. This is a call to forsake everything and deliver everything and everyone up to the King. It is written…

> "Thou hast ravished my heart, my sister, my spouse; thou hast ravished my heart with one of thine eyes, with one chain of thy neck." Song of Solomon 4:9

The call is clear and unrelenting. It is the call to fellowship with the King which is what the weary intercessor has been seeking for such a long time. The question is, will this one pay the price of dying to self, self will, self desires, for the holy fellowship with the King which He now offers?

Practical Exercise

A hungering soul with a deep desire for intercession or one who has been an intercessor may believe that he/she is ready for this deeper level of intercession—and that one may be almost ready. However, because this is such a high calling, stop here and prepare yourself to take the first step into the covenant signed earlier..

> *Obtain a copy of the book,* ***The Inner Court Ministry: With Christ the Master Teacher in the School of Prayer,"*** *by Pernell H. Hewing, Ph.D, Th.D*

Put this book aside and read, study, and pray through the Inner Court Ministry...

Meet with the Lord at least three times a week for approximately 30 minutes for this exercise. Spend as much time as necessary on each chapter. Make notes of what God reveals to you at the end of your meeting time with the Lord.

*Pray and reread the **Inner Court Ministry** information. Read carefully and slowly. Read a paragraph slowly, then pray the paragraph for yourself.*

Notes

CHAPTER 8

THE *KINGDOM INTERCESSOR* IS A "HIDDEN ONE"

The Ministry of **Kingdom Intercession** brings the intercessor into that true hidden life with the King. *The intercessor becomes a hidden one and the hidden one learns deeper and deeper secrets of the Ministry of **Kingdom Intercession*** which is carried on all in the name of Jesus Christ, the name of the King, and is effective only on the ground of death to self. The **Kingdom Intercessor** says ...

> *"I am crucified with Christ; nevertheless I live; yet not I, but Christ liveth in me: and the life which I now live in the flesh I live by the faith of the Son of God, who loved me, and gave himself for me." Galatians 2:20*

The **Kingdom Intercessor** needs to know that the Ministry of **Kingdom Intercession** is effective on the grounds of resurrection in the Lord Jesus...

> *"For if we have been planted together in the likeness of his death, we shall be also in the likeness of his resurrection:" Romans 6:5*

The ***Kingdom Intercessor*** learns that Ministry of ***Kingdom Intercession*** is entrusted to the intercessor. The King says to His ***Kingdom Intercessor***...

> *"Verily I say unto you, Whatsoever ye shall bind on earth shall be bound in heaven: and whatsoever ye shall loose on earth shall be loosed in heaven." Matt. 18:18*

The ***Kingdom Intercessor*** comes to know that the Ministry of ***Kingdom Intercession*** is affected by the head of the church, the Lord Jesus, because the Father...

> *"...hath put all things under his feet, and gave him to be the head over all things to the church,*
>
> *"Which is his body, the fullness of him that filleth all in all." Ephesians 1:22-23*

The Ministry of ***Kingdom Intercession*** is carried out all in the name of the King, the Lord Jesus Christ. The intercessor, the hidden one, serves Him, the great King Jesus, and knows and has heard His call. It is written...

> *"And from Jesus Christ, who is the faithful witness, and the first begotten of the dead, and the prince of the kings of the earth. Unto him that loved us and washed us from our sins in his own blood,*
>
> *"And hath made us kings and priests unto God and his Father; to him be glory and dominion for ever and ever Amen." Revelation 1:5-6*

The Hidden life of the *Kingdom Intercessor*

To become the "hidden one" with the King is to enter into covenant with the Lord Jesus to accept the call to the ministry of **Kingdom Intercession**. The ministry of **Kingdom Intercession** is the ministry of and for the Body of Christ for the hidden ones. The call to the position of a "Hidden One" is the call to intimacy. It is the call to a covenant relationship, and a call to covenant. It is a call to a covenant relationship with Jesus Christ, the King.

Kingdom Intercession is the work of the Hidden Ones

The King does everything by covenant and one must enter into the covenant with the King. This covenant becomes the wedding garment which will bring one into the covenant relationship with King Jesus. This is not a small, insignificant thing. The Ministry of **Kingdom Intercession** is the work of the "called out" one -- the hidden one.

Kingdom Intercession is the work of the **Kingdom Intercessor** of Christ, the King. However, "... *many are called, but few are chosen.*" Matthew 22:14. The **Kingdom Intercessor** is a hidden one in covenant with the King and he/she is now a member of ...

> "... *a chosen generation, a royal priesthood, an holy nation, a peculiar people; that ye should show forth the praises of him who hath called you out of darkness into his marvellous light:*" I Peter 2:9

It is the covenant relationship, the position of the hidden one, which brings one to the chosen for **Kingdom Intercession**. Salvation opens the way to the call to **Kingdom Intercessor**, but it is the fulfillment of the requirements for intercession which brings one to **Kingdom Intercession**. Having come to this place with the King, the **Kingdom Intercessor** knows that Jesus gives the *anointing* of power in prayer and delegates authority for answers to prayer.

The Ultimate Power for Answers in Prayer

The *anointing* of power for answers in prayer abides in the believer as it is imparted by God as one walks in all the revealed will of God. As one obeys what God reveals as he/she prays and enters into the Word of God as led by the Holy Ghost, that one's body becomes the temple of the Holy Ghost. The believer then receives power in his/her body by virtue of the fact that authority has been delegated to him/her to pray in that authority and the authority of power is given for answers to prayer at that level.

The body of the believer walking in delegated authority and power becomes the reservoir for the *anointing*. That earthen vessel carries the treasure of the anointed power of God. The anointed power the believer carries in his/her body to work the works of God will....

> *"Heal the sick, cleanse the lepers, ... cast out devils: freely ye have received, freely give."* Matthew 10:8

In covenant to become **Kingdom Intercessor** for the King, one is committed to remain steadfast until death just as in marriage one is committed to remain steadfast until death. That is why a formal covenant must precede entrance into the ministry of *Kingdom Intercession*. The *Kingdom Intercessor* is signing up for a royal battle because the enemy knows the power that will come against him when the *Kingdom Intercessor* matures and moves into his/her position.

As Jesus Christ is the King of the Kingdom of Heaven, He calls His *Kingdom Intercessors* to surrender all for this call. The call is the call for laying down one's life on order to open the way for the Kingdom of Heaven to come in the earth as it is in Heaven. Anything short of total commitment to the King and to the Kingdom closes the door of entrance into the ministry of *Kingdom Intercession*.

One Must Make a New Covenant to Enter the Ministry of *Kingdom Intercession*

To become a *Kingdom Intercessor*, one must enter into a covenant with the Lord to pay the price for entrance. Until one chooses to undergo the process which brings one into this all-important position, that one is standing outside a covenant position — the position where the Lord can truly use him/her in *Kingdom Intercession*. That one then will not be in position to participate in the all-important movement where the Lord is using His intercessor.

A Microscopic Look at Covenant

A covenant is an alliance of friendship between individuals: a pledge or agreement with obligations between a superior God and an inferior man, a constitution between God and man. A covenant is a pact or agreement between two or more parties. It may be an agreement to which parties voluntarily come to accept stipulation of the tenets of the covenant. Covenant is accompanied by signs, sacrifices, and a oath that seals it with promises or blessings for keeping the covenant, and curses for breaking the covenant.

God's actions are linked to a covenant, and that covenant is between God and man. The Lord, therefore, is calling His believers to make that once-and-for-all-time decision to make a covenant to enter into *Kingdom Intercession* to become His intercessor. It is time for the believer to sanctify self unto the Lord and decide if he/she will accept the call to *Kingdom Intercession* in the Kingdom of Heaven and live out Kingdom principles on earth.

The Midnight Hour Approaches

The midnight hour approaches when He, whom the soul loves, is to appear. Soon Jesus Christ, whom we serve and to whom we belong, will come. It is time to leave everything behind to follow Him. It is time to sanctify yourself unto Him now and enter into the ministry of the Royal Priesthood, the invincible army of the Lord, and the Vanguard of the Saints Movement.

The believer is in the midnight hour in preparation for the End-time Battle of the Age. It is no longer a time to learn more to help one in a ministry or to help one grow in the Lord. NOT SO!!! It is now time for a final decision because God is calling the believer/saints to *Kingdom Intercession*.

Practical Exercises
Covenant Agreement Prayer

*Lord, I will to be your **Kingdom Intercessor** and am willing to become the **Kingdom Intercessor** of Christ. I cannot become your **Kingdom Intercessor** on my own strength, but I can do the following three things and will do them.*

I CAN ... choose to enter into and complete the Practical exercises as directed.

I CAN ... PRAY; that is, I can keep asking the King for help.

*I CAN ... choose to enter into the covenant for **Kingdom Intercessor** with the King and I believe that I can trust The King to perfect that which concerns me.*

Write additional covenant promises in your prayer notebook if necessary:

Name _____
Date:_____

Practical Exercise
To Begin *Kingdom Intercession*

To become the anointed **Kingdom Intercessor** *with a passion, one needs take to take as much time in preparation as necessary. Pause here and prepare to move in deeper into the different levels.*

The King wants to establish **Kingdom Intercessors** *for corporate jet-like fast and powerful answers to prayer. The preparation helps one to be able to come into His Holy hill and abide in his presence. Perhaps that is why He has asked the question in Psalms 15: "Who shall abide in thy tabernacle? Who shall dwell in thy holy hill?" Psalms 15:1*

Many may be anxious to begin praying for the specific. However, the King calls to another time of preparation. Begin by consecrating self over Psalms 15, 24, and 25.

Where to begin? *Every verse of Psalms 15 must be entered into and lived by each person who is preparing for* **Kingdom Intercessor***. This may take weeks.*

Directive: This is very serious intercession. The Lord says..."if you be willing and obedient, ye shall eat the good of the land:" Isaiah 1:19

The call is to commit to be faithful to meet with the Lord one or two times a week 5:30 a.m. to 6:30 a.m. or some early morning hour that is convenient.

During the a.m. hour chosen for meeting, pray in the Spirit, but most of one's prayer will be the Word of God. PRAY PSALMS 15 AND PSALMS 24.

One cannot approach the Lord without the blood of Jesus as token. It is written…"…the priest went always into the first tabernacle, accomplishing the service of God.

"But into the second went the high priest alone…NOT WITHOUT BLOOD, which he offered for himself, and for the errors of the people." Heb. 9:6-7

Each time one meets the King, one will also take communion.

DIRECTIONS FOR PRAYER TIME: When one meets for intercession, begin with a brief time of praise, honor, thanksgiving and worship. Read, meditate, and pray Psalms 15. Use verses for examination and repentance.

After a time of examination and repentance, TAKE COMMUNION. One may spend days with one verse of Psalms 15—beginning with verse 1. To allow time for the King's examination before taking communion, pray, meditate and/or set self to do whatever the verse directs.

After communion, move into intercession and begin reading through Psalms 24. Then go back and meditate on each verse so that the Lord can give you revelation knowledge for this Intercession. Psalms 24 has 10 verses.

Pray, meditate, believe, declare and set self to do what the verse says.

Spend consecrated time with the prayer. Wait quietly for God to speak, and write what the Lord reveals.

BONUS PRAYER: Pray the following prayer regularly.

"Lord, cleanse my mind, my heart, and my spirit and renew me by your Spirit and keep my inner most being cleansed and fresh.

"Root out every evil thought and every erroneous thought toward God, people, and towards myself. Root out all religious, unholy, and selfish notions so that what I believe is completely of God."

"Lord, make me real before you, before people, and real with myself. Help me to know the truth that the truth will make me free."

Second part of the hour, move to Psalms 24 or 25. Use the same procedures used in Ps. 15. DON'T RUSH.

CHAPTER 9

THE CALL NOW IS PERSONAL...
ARE YOU READY TO ANSWER THE CALL?

You are being called now to make a decision for this deeper life.

> *Are you ready for complete, no-compromise surrender?*
> *Are you ready for this?*

The call to enter into the ministry of *Kingdom Intercession* is a call to answer the call and take your position in **Kingdom Intercession**. It is different from the call to prayer. It is a call to unconditional surrender of life and everything which pertains to your life. It is a call to **Kingdom Intercession** and Kingdom living. It is the true calling to enter into the fullness of the intercession and to position yourself to be the Vanguard of intercession for the King. You are being called now to make a decision for this deeper life:

> *Are you ready for complete, no-compromise surrender?*
> *Are you ready for this?*

This call to **Kingdom Intercession** is a high *Priestly* call. The scriptures in the Old Testament show that the priesthood is a group of people wholly separated from the world in order to serve God and serve in the presence of the Lord. The call to the ministry of **Kingdom Intercession** is a call to a pure *Priestly* ministry before the Lord. When the

Lord calls one to be his *Kingdom Intercessor*, it is a call to survival in the End-time Battle of the Age.

> *Are you ready for this total commitment?*

Even if intercessors believe that their past work and ministry in intercession have thrust them and anchored them securely forever into the ministry of intercession, the call now to the ministry of *Kingdom Intercession* is a call for the awesome task of entering into the invincible army of the King for the End-time Battle of the Age.

The call to the ministry of the End-time Royal Priesthood is a call to forget everything and everyone, leave everything behind, and find delight in the Lord and Savior, Jesus Christ.

> *Are you ready for this? It is written...*
> *"... many are called, but few are chosen." Matt. 22:14*

It is a decision-making time. From this point, one must go deeper and decide if he/she is willing to go all the way. Here one has come to the point of no return. The time is past for one to glean more information to enjoy or to hope to get help for self. The call to the ministry of the *Kingdom Intercession* is a call to sincere believers to come into position with the Lord where the Lord can tell that one what to do and he/she will do it, and then God will do what He and He alone can do.

> *Are you ready to choose now this ministry, serving always around the throne of the Lord?*

The one who chooses to say "yes" to the ministry of **Kingdom Intercessor** cannot wander in and out of the Spirit, but must live and walk in the Spirit at all times. The call to the ministry of **Kingdom Intercession** is a call into the forefront of the battle for the King to come. It begins with intimacy with Jesus Christ as the **Kingdom Intercessor** is called to come into a position with God to touch the heart of God and pray through and work out that which touches the heart of God.

> *Are you ready for this total commitment?*

Fleshly desires must be nailed to the cross, good and noble deeds must be put to rest, and religious activities must be sanctified and made spiritual. Many will need to be stopped, and some will be modified. This is not a call to the ministry only nor to church work. This is about a life totally given over to the LORD for His use.

> *Are you ready for this total commitment?*

Too few of God's children choose to pay the price for this coveted position of the ministry of **Kingdom Intercession**. Too many spend their Christian life wandering around partially or fully blinded to God and His magnificent glory because they have not come close enough to touch or experience Him. The called-out **Kingdom Intercessor** who answers the call will experience and touch God.

> *Are you ready for this total commitment?*

The call to the ministry of *Kingdom Intercession* is a special call, and the call to be an Intercessor for the King is even more special. It is the highest calling in the Kingdom of Heaven. Many miss this wonderful privilege because they are not willing to pay the price, not sure of the call, and/or are not ready to pay the price to enter this calling.

> *Are You Ready to Give Up Everything for this Call — Fame, Recognition--a MINISTRY, Everything?*

Greater is the call to be a *Kingdom Intercessor* than any other call upon one's life because God the Father has called as many as will for this great calling to fulfill a special work He has in His heart. This is a great blessing for the one who answers this call, but one must choose to return not to a slippery Christian walk.

> *Are you willing to pray here and ask God to show you your former slippery Christian walk?*

When He reveals your slippery Christian walk, are you willing to listen to what He says, and choose to give up one thing at a time, one-by-one? The call to the ministry of *Kingdom Intercession* is a spiritual calling, and one must enter into it in the Spirit, by the Spirit and through the Spirit. It is too gigantic a call to enter in by one's own strength — one must depend on God totally. That means total unconditional commitment to God and deep cleansing, deep healing, and great deliverance for the one called. Again...

"... many are called, but few are chosen." Matt. 22:14

Many born-again believers are called to the ministry of Intercession, but few are chosen for the ministry of *Kingdom Intercession*. This is a very serious call and carries a heavy requirement. Before one says 'yes' to this calling, one will surely need to count the cost. The *Kingdom Intercessor* gives up every aspect of life for this call, just as Jesus Christ, the High Priest, gave His life for the believer's salvation.

Are you ready for this total commitment?

The cost of the ministry of *Kingdom Intercession* is death to self and every desire for self. It requires death to life as one knows it, and death to one's desires, ambitions, hopes, dreams. The *Kingdom Intercessor* enters directly into the presence of the Lord as he/she serves around the throne in the presence of the Lord.

Are you ready to give up everything for this call—fame, recognition, A MINISTRY--Everything?

The call to the ministry of *Kingdom Intercession* in the Kingdom of Heaven is a call to be separated unto the Lord and dedicated to His service. It means that one is in the world, but not of the world. It means that all one does is done unto the Lord and that one has his/her being in Jesus

Christ. It means that one is taught of the Lord and that one is for the Lord in all things.

> *It is time to make that decision here and now, never to take it back. Are you ready?*

The ***Kingdom Intercessor*** will pay the same price for the ministry of ***Kingdom Intercession*** that Jesus Christ paid for mankind. The Father had to send His only Son, and the blood that the Son shed was needed to save the whole world. The life that one gives up will be for the Kingdom of Heaven. It will put one out front in the End-time Battle of the Kingdom of Heaven.

> *Are you ready to pay the price? Are you ready for this total commitment?*

The conditions of one's life and the things happening around one and the distance many saints are from the Lord require more than prayers that may or may not reach heaven. It requires a life given over so completely to the ministry of Intercession that nothing else matters. The call is to the ministry of ***Kingdom Intercession*** for the Kingdom.

> *Are you ready for this mighty call, and the price you will have to pay for Kingdom Intercession?*

It is time now to make the once-for-all-time commitment to take your position as a ***Kingdom Intercessor*** and enter into the ministry of ***Kingdom***

Intercession. That can only be done when one gives his/her life to the ministry of **Kingdom Intercession**.

> *Are you ready to make that decision here, now, never to take it back? — Are you ready?*

One must decide if his/her lifestyle and life's work require too much of one's time to make this type of commitment. One must choose to make a commitment and pay the price for **Kingdom Intercession**. The call to the ministry of **Kingdom Intercessor** is not only to pray, but also to come in position with the Captain of the Lord of Hosts so that He can give the **Kingdom Intercessor** the battle-plan for the battle. The call is to **Kingdom Intercession**, the Vanguard for the Kingdom of Heaven. This is going to require fasting, praying, searching God's Word, and claiming the promises.

> *It is time to make that decision here now, never to take it back. Are you ready?*

The one who says 'yes' to this call to the ministry of **Kingdom Intercession** of the Kingdom of Heaven must know the requirements and be willing to meet the requirements. This call will of necessity require searching one's own heart and examining one's own life, one's ways, and one's behavior. It is going to require a holy, committed life.

> *Are you ready for this deep spiritual walk and deep spiritual life?*

Because this is such a special call and the promise is to the *Kingdom Intercessor* if he/she will rise to the call, one needs to make a formal commitment to the Lord and enter into a covenant agreement with God and others to continue to the end.

> *It is time to make that decision here now, never to take it back. Are you ready?*

This is a call that will not make one popular or help one gain favor in the ministry. Instead, it will call one to give up ministries and much activity in the religious arena in order to spend more time with the Master in Intercession.

> *Time to make that decision here and now, never to take it back. Are you ready?*

Kingdom Intercessors are Priests unto the Lord. The scriptures reveal that the Priests lived their lives separated from loved ones, misunderstood, and abused, but they loved and obeyed God's Word. They lived a life of prayer and praise, and they offered burnt offerings making intercession for the people. As a *Kingdom Intercessor* of the Kingdom of Heaven, one will stand before the Lord in intercession, warring and serving as a watchman.

> *It is time to make that decision here now, never to take it back. Are you ready?*

Practical Exercise

*Acceptance to the call to enter into the ministry of **Kingdom Intercession** in and for the Kingdom of Heaven brings one to the call into Kingdom living. Now is the time to make one's election for the Kingdom of Heaven sure and to take the **Priestly** position of **Kingdom Intercessor**. Begin by completing the following Practical Exercise.*

*This is a serious assignment to help one decide if he/she wants to enter into the Ministry of **Kingdom Intercession** for the King. The prayers one is called to pray in this position will not be ordinary praying, nor will one be praying when he/she is ready or when he/she feels like it. The one who chooses to enter into this ministry of **Kingdom Intercession** will spend his/her life praying around the throne as the Lord leads.*

<u>DIRECTIONS:</u> *Reread this information paying special attention to the questions enclosed in boxes throughout the information. Go back and reread the paragraph(s) before each box. Pray each one several times. Pray in the spirit and ask the Lord to reveal to you the following:*

What is the cost of answering the call, and what does the call mean when you answer 'yes' to the question? Make a list of all the Lord reveals to you.

Pray the question again for the Lord to reveal to you what you have to give up if you answer the call.

COVENANT AND PRAY FOR ENTERING INTO THE MINISTRY OF *KINGDOM INTERCESSION*

It is a decision-making time. From this point, one must go deeper and choose if he/she is willing to go all the way. We have come to the point of no return.

The time is past for one to glean more information to enjoy or to hope to get help for self. The time is now for total, unconditional surrender.

Spend a week praying and/or writing your covenant of intercession. If you want to sign the covenant below, read it and pray. Pray it each time you meet with the Lord. If you want to write your own, write it and sign it. Have it witnessed by someone in spiritual authority.

If you want to use the Covenant below, read and reread it and sign it as your covenant with THE KING.

KINGDOM INTERCESSION COVENANT AGREEMENT

Lord, I, _____ covenant with you this day (date) _____ to enter into the call into greater service--the call to the New Beginning of **Kingdom Intercession**. I hereby answer the call to intercession.

I choose to begin whatever is necessary to become a **Kingdom Intercessor** for the King. I promise to prepare myself as is suggested in this book to become a **Kingdom Intercessor**.

I accept the call to let the King be everything in my life. I abandon myself to the King. I accept the call to be **Kingdom Intercessor**. I commit myself today, my Lord and Master, to take my position with Christ as an Intercessor. I promise not to strain nor strive. I will cast myself on the King and know that then and only then will I have the full power of the Spirit operating within me.

I will press on toward the fullness of the call to **Kingdom Intercession** with the King. I will forsake family and other loved ones if called by you to do so. I will love The Lord more than myself.

Dear Lord, I promise to come to the King regularly to sup with Him, to sit in His presence, to learn from the King and to spend consecrated time with The King. I will not boast in self, in anyone or anything except Jesus Christ.

I will not count myself more than Jesus. I will remember that The King is the source of everything -- that He is first and will always be first in my life. I will have no other god before the King. I will praise the King, worship, love, honor, obey, thank, and trust Him.

Write on a separate sheet any additional promises to God you desire to make.

Signed _____ Date _____

Address _____ Ph _____

City, State _____ Zip _____

Witness _____ Title _____

PART III

THE END-TIME *KINGDOM INTERCESSOR* CALLED TO THE FOREFRONT OF...

Finally, my brethren, be strong in the Lord and in the power of his might.

"Put on the whole armour of God, that ye may be able to stand against the wiles of the devil."
Ephesians 6:10-11

STRATOSPHERIC WARFARE AND

KINGDOM INTERCESSION

TO

Wins the Battle...

...For the King of kings and Lord of lords

Chapter 10

The *Kingdom Intercessor* Called to Stratospheric Warfare

The *Kingdom Intercessor* is called to spiritual warfare because satan is waging a battle for control, and the battle is for control of the saints/believers and the Church. The battlefront is the Church, the home, the nations, the state, and the community. The mature *Kingdom Intercessor* is called to this battlefront. The prepared *Kingdom Intercessor* will take this battle beyond prayer, because that one will know that his/her call is not to petition God because God has already been given the weapons to win the battle.

The trained and prepared *Kingdom Intercessors* will go out on the battlefield knowing that the Captain of the Lord's host has defeated satan and that they have ultimate authority to take back what has been stolen by satan. With authoritative prayer, the *Kingdom Intercessor* will command whatever hinders to stop, will bind evil spirits, will loose the Holy Spirit, and will halt the activities of satan.

The *Kingdom Intercessor* will bring the power of authoritative prayer to the Church which will rend the heavens and tear down the strongholds which have been over the Church and which have hindered the Church from fulfilling its call to greatness. The mature *Kingdom Intercessors* will enter into God's power because they will know God.

It is written…

"But unto you that fear my name shall the Sun of righteousness arise with healing in his wings; and ye shall go forth, and grow up as calves of the stall.

"And ye shall tread down the wicked; for they shall be ashes under the soles of your feet in the day that I shall do this, saith the LORD of hosts."
Malachi 4:2-3

Satan has special interest in the Church; therefore, the battle is on for the Church and for God's people because satan knows that his time is short. The battle is fierce because of the hidden missiles satan has in place through strongholds in the believer and in the Church. These strongholds must be identified and pulled down, and the prepared *Kingdom Intercessors* will be equipped to find these hidden missiles of satan.

The End-time *Kingdom Intercessors* will battle the power of darkness against satan's control over the Church. Satan will do everything in his power to sidetrack, hinder, weaken, and destroy the Church's ministry. Satan fights to keep God's ways and God's desires out of the Church and to plant his own.

Kingdom Intercessors Confronts Personal Strongholds and Strongholds in the Church

Strongholds the *Kingdom Intercessors* must pull down are fleshly centers of control of the person's thoughts, feelings, and actions. This is where *Kingdom Intercessors* will be called to a difficult and treacherous battle, because these centers are deeply entrenched in individuals and must be delivered before the Church can be delivered out of the hands of satan.

THE *KINGDOM INTERCESSORS* WILL PULL DOWN STRONGHOLDS AND UNCOVER SATAN'S HIDDEN MISSILES

NOTE THE FOLLOWING ILLUSTRATION

Strongholds...

SATAN'S Hidden Missiles

Strongholds are fleshly centers for control of the person's THOUGHTS ... FEELINGS ... ACTIONS
A home for **CONTROLLING SPIRITS**

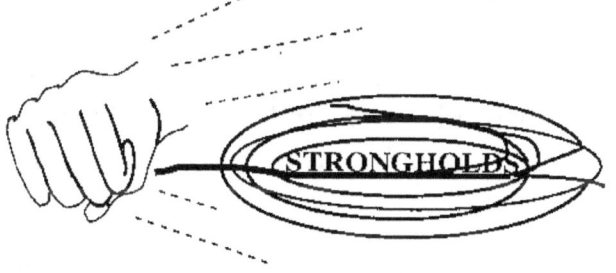

"(For the weapons of our warfare are not carnal, but mighty through God to the pulling down of strong holds)."
II Corinthians 10:4

Kingdom Intercessors Confronts Personal Strongholds and Strongholds in the Church

Strongholds the *Kingdom Intercessors* must pull down are fleshly centers of control of the person's thoughts, feelings, and actions. This is where *Kingdom Intercessors* will be called to a difficult and treacherous battle, because these centers are deeply entrenched in individuals and must be delivered before the Church can be delivered out of the hands of satan. Personal strongholds in one's life may be difficult to uncover and even more difficult to haul to the cross where they must be taken. These strongholds may have a strangle hold on one's innermost being because self is attached to the stronghold, and self must choose to die.

It is important for the *Kingdom Intercessors* to deal with personal strongholds before dealing with the strongholds over the Church, over cities, and over nations. The enemy may have captured the individual through strongholds, but that is not the end of it. To capture the army of the Lord, the enemy sets out to build strongholds within the believer/saint, and within the Body of Christ, often using strongholds in and over individuals. Many of the strongholds are brought in through cultural mores, traditions, religion, etc.

Much work may be done to tear down the strongholds in the individual saints, but the stronghold over the Body of Christ and through the Church may be missed. They can easily be missed because they are inextricably interwoven into the very fabric of the doctrine or the tradition or the culture of the individuals in the Church. These are satan's hidden missiles.

Kingdom Intercessors Must Overcome Strongholds over the Church

Strongholds over the Church are under the control of the world rulers of the darkness, and this is the greatest threat to the Body of Christ. Satan's strongholds hypnotize the believers and produce a spell which overshadows them. This clouds the Word of God or the truths that might set them free. The enemy then prevents the individual and the Church from overcoming the power of the strongholds.

Strongholds put up smoke screens using multifarious tactics to block truths. These strongholds will prevent one from hearing sermons, teaching, counseling and words of wisdom which will set the listener free. These tactics are used to keep the believer from repentance and freedom. They put up a protective shield around the untruth that keeps one in bondage to lies and in bondage to self and flesh.

The tactics strongholds use to shield the believer from truth also keep a Church or a body of believers in bondage to lies and deception. These satanic strongholds produce speculations—things raised against the knowledge of God—and cause one NOT to take thoughts captive and bring them into obedience to Christ. It is written...

> *"(For the weapons of our warfare are not carnal, but mighty through God to the pulling down of strong holds;)*
>
> *"Casting down imaginations, and every high thing that exalteth itself against the knowledge of God, and bringing into captivity every thought to the obedience of Christ;"* II Corinthians 10:4-5

Demons and Principalities Rule Strongholds

Satan will use mental strongholds over individuals and over a group to control individuals, churches, groups and nations through the use of demons and principalities. The purpose of the stronghold is to protect against outsiders' thoughts, influences, etc. Satan's strategic purpose is to prevent individuals from seeing and knowing the truth, and the spirit behind the stronghold keeps the individual from seeing his/her own deception.

Strongholds should be obvious to the casual observer; however, strongholds will narrow one's vision to prevent that one from seeing what common sense would show is wrong. The stronghold will enter into one's innermost thoughts and become a part of his/her thought pattern, and the believer is then captured by satan and is then bound to his/her deception.

These are personal strongholds, and they are very dangerous. They gather thoughts and fleshly habits and lies which hold one captive and cause that one to believe the lies to be truths. That is why this battle is not against demons only, but a power greater and more difficult to uncover. For victory, the *Kingdom Intercessor* must not just give attention to defeating the demons, but must uncover and pull down the ruling spirit.

Strongholds influence Culture and Prevent a People Group

Strongholds over a Church, body of people, a culture, a people group, etc. form blockages that are almost impossible to demolish causing deceitful ways of thinking, feeling, and acting i.e., a following a particular code of behavior, i.e. a dress code peculiar to that body of people. Therefore, the stronghold has built into that group a common mentality, a common way of thinking. This stronghold has spun lies and half truths which are shared by that body or Church or group, and members of the group believe the lies. These lies are pitted against God to be truth.

When a stronghold has been established in a Church or group, this becomes the common thought pattern of the body of people. As a part of that Church or body of believers or group, it becomes the thought pattern of individuals in that group also. That pattern of thoughts is pitted against the ways of Jesus Christ and must be torn down so that one has only the mind of Christ.

Corporate Strongholds Hinder a Church

Corporate strongholds in a Church are built and strengthened from deception and ways of thinking long practiced by the group. In a Church or a body of people, the enemy sets up strongholds composed of <u>philosophies, rituals, traditions, cultural behavior, practices and values.</u> It is so easy for one to fall into the practices. Members within the group are bound to these lies in what encompasses the group, individuals do not realize that they have embraced these unholy behavior and thought patterns common to the group.

The <u>traditions, rituals, behaviors,</u> etc. that are common practices fueled by the stronghold in a Church, body of people, or a group were part of the old life of the individuals, and they feel comfortable in them. Oftentimes a leader that has long left the scene brought the practices into the spiritual life.

By the time strongholds in a Church or group are discerned, they are so deeply entrenched in the people that they are difficult to detect and even more difficult to pull down. One will not be able to pull them down unless one detects his/her own strongholds and pull them down.

The End-time *Kingdom Intercessors* are called to win the battle against corporate strongholds in order to take deliverance to its higher purpose. The corporate strongholds are operated by principalities, rulers, and demonic powers to imprison the minds and control the thoughts of an entire group of people in local Churches and entire denominations. The purpose of these strongholds is to prevent one from thinking for him/herself and to prevent the individual from accepting truths and logic contrary to the mindset of the stronghold.

THE LORD CAN SHINE LIGHT ON STRONGHOLDS

As the *Kingdom Intercessor* draws closer to the Lord, he/she can see and discern an unholy stronghold, but may not understand clearly the depths of the stronghold. They may be tempted to walk away, calling much of what seen as legalism, religion, or a cultural mindset.

Legalistic behavior from the culture may be a manifestation, but the stronghold is the hidden missile of satan, the center of which is religion controlled by a religious demon. The End-time *Kingdom Intercessor* who has overcome personal strongholds will be prepared to identify the hidden missiles of satan in the Church and to tear down these strongholds. *Kingdom Intercessors* will be given the authority against which satan cannot stand. As the *Kingdom Intercessor* comes to maturity and into covenant, he/she will step into the authority given by God for this battle and stay in a position with the Lord that the Lord can tell him/her what to do, and he/she will do it; and then God will do what is necessary to win the battle.

When the End-time *Kingdom Intercessor* comes into his/her maturity and positions him/herself with God through covenant-making for this battle, that one will know how to stand in a position of victory over the strongholds of satan in the Church. In this battle, one needs the authority of a general, not that of a foot soldier.

For this End-time Battle of the Age, the Lord is trying to prepare the *Kingdom Intercessors* and crown them with power and authority to bring the Church to victory. *Kingdom Intercessors*, therefore, must be willing to prepare to tear down these invisible strongholds satan has set in the Body of Christ as his hidden missiles. This is not only a work for generals, majors, and captains, but also the work of the BELIEVERS/SAINTS who are called to the ministry of *Kingdom Intercession*.

The *Kingdom Intercessor* must declare war against wickedness and must prepare themselves, because the battle will be fierce. The war the *Kingdom Intercessor* must fight is the battle between Jesus, the Holy Spirit, and the Word of God. They must fight against satan, wickedness, and evil spirits. Jesus wills the **Kingdom Intercessor** the gift of authoritative prayer, therefore, when they come to the battlefield, the **Kingdom Intercessors** will know that they are not operating in their strength, but operating via the throne.

The Kingdom Intercessor Must declare WAR

On Unrighteousness and Wickedness

CHAPTER 11

THE *KINGDOM INTERCESSOR* UNITES WITH THE LORD OF HOSTS FOR VICTORY

King Jesus calls the *Kingdom Intercessor* to say, *"Ready or not, here I come."* Because the *Kingdom Intercessor* may be so far away from maturity, he/she may be still hiding out, knowing that he/she has a ministry of deliverance for the Body of Christ, but thinking he/she is not ready. The door swings wide to that one now to come forth and prepare for that ministry. He/she is beckoned to come to **The King of kings,** the *Lord of Hosts*—the Lord who delivers. His name is now Jesus and it was written of Him...

"...For this purpose the Son of God was manifested, that he might destroy the works of the devil." I John 3:8(b)

Jesus said of Himself...

"The Spirit of the Lord is upon me, because he hath anointed me to preach the gospel to the poor; he hath sent me to heal the brokenhearted, to preach deliverance to the captives, and recovering of sight to the blind, to set at liberty them that are bruised," Luke 4:18

The call of the Lord Jesus Christ to the **Kingdom Intercessor** is so crucial at this time because the Kingdom of Heaven is at hand, and the **Kingdom Intercessor** is called to governmental leadership for and in the kingdom. The End-time **Kingdom Intercessor**, therefore, must enter into union with the King of kings and the Lord of lords.

The ministry of **Kingdom Intercession** is a ministry assigned by the King of kings and Lord of lords; however, many called **Kingdom Intercessors**, though born of the Spirit of the living God, have not reached maturity. Perhaps they are afraid to answer the call because they need healing and deliverance, but will not submit themselves for their healing and/or deliverance. Is the Lord not healing and delivering today?

The Lord beckons the End-time **Kingdom Intercessor** to come for deliverance and to allow Him to put the ministry of deliverance into their hands to take to a world bound by the power of darkness. The King of kings speaks from heaven that this End-time **Kingdom Intercession** ministry is a ministry where one meets a sovereign ruler of heaven and earth who comes down to deliver and set free.

When one answers the call to **Kingdom Intercession**, one meets the *Lord of Hosts* who heals and delivers. When the End-time **Kingdom Intercessor** reaches maturity, he/she will know that the battle is the Lord's, and He will give the enemy into that one's hands by His divine might and power.

Until the End-time **Kingdom Intercessor** reaches maturity, he/she falls back into the spirit of self and the old man and the corrupt nature dominate. If the End-time *Kingdom Intercessor* comes to the King of kings when in the midst of a struggle and with his/her own inadequate resources, that one can know that one can be delivered from the wiles of the enemy. It is written...

> *"...the Son of God (Jesus) was manifested, that he might destroy the works of the devil."* I John 3:8(b)

Since Jesus Christ was manifested to destroy the works of the devil and He has come to bring the Kingdom of Heaven to earth, He equips the End-time *Kingdom Intercessor* to destroy all the strongholds that satan has built into one's life before he/she became a believer. If these strongholds are not destroyed, they will overcome the End-time *Kingdom Intercessor*, but he/she will overcome at last as he/she unites with the King.

For the walls of strongholds to come down, the End-time *Kingdom Intercessor* will fight battles with the enemy, satan, which will lead to intense warfare. When the battle is over, the Kingdom of Heaven will be established on earth in the hearts of the people of God. The King of the Kingdom, the Lord Jesus Christ, is the means of defense, It is written...

> *"For though we walk in the flesh, we do not war after the flesh:*
>
> *"(For the weapons of our warfare are not carnal, but mighty through God to the pulling down of strong holds;)*
>
> *"Casting down imaginations, and every high thing that exalteth itself against the knowledge of God, and*

bringing into captivity every thought to the obedience of Christ;

"And having in a readiness to revenge all disobedience, when your obedience is fulfilled." II Corinthians 10:3-6

The End-time **Kingdom Intercessor** needs to know that he/she is righteous; that is, that he/she is in right standing with the Lord God of the Universe. As the End-time **Kingdom Intercessor** prepares for governmental leadership in the Kingdom, that one needs to know that he/she stands secure as the righteous. Then the King of the Universe releases His power through that righteous one.

The mature End-time **Kingdom Intercessor** is the righteous one who can trust in the name of the Lord Jesus. The righteous ones have put their trust in Jesus Christ for salvation; that is, trusted Jesus to be his/her savior from an eternal death. That one is now counted as righteous son or daughter, and all power is available to them. It is written...

"But as many as received him, to them gave he power to become the sons of God, even to them that believe on his name:" John 1:12

The mature **Kingdom Intercessor** is the one who has entered into the covenant of grace; that is, has accepted Jesus Christ as savior, made him Lord and Master of his/her life, and chose to become a bond-slave to Jesus, the righteous one. This act puts one in right relationship with God as it establishes a deeper covenant with the Master and a closer bond to God the Father. One can then be positioned as End-time **Kingdom Intercessor**.

The enemy can defeat the **Kingdom Intercessor** although he/she is righteous if the righteous one is not firmly established in who he/she is in Christ and doesn't believe in the power in the name of his/her savior, Jesus Christ. However, the End-time **Kingdom Intercessor** who is prepared for governmental leadership in the Kingdom will know that he/she can run into the name of the Lord Jesus—the banner for the Kingdom of Heaven—and be safe. The name of the Lord is great among the heathen and dreadful. It is written…

"…I am a great King, saith the LORD of hosts, and my name is dreadful among the heathen." Malachi 1:14b

When **Kingdom Intercessors** are secure in their position of righteousness and find themselves failing and are impotent in the face of unbearable trials, they can then run into the name of their King, the Lord of Hosts, safely boasting in that name. It is written…

"Some trust in chariots, and some in horses: but we will remember the name of the LORD our God.

"They are brought down and fallen: but we are risen, and stand upright." Psalms 20:7-8

As the **Kingdom Intercessor**, the End-time pastor, the minister, or leader, come forth, he/she will find that… *"The name of the Lord is a strong tower: the righteous runneth into it, and is safe…"* This is where the End-time **Kingdom Intercessor** runs for victory over the enemy because this is the only place where victory can be found.

Before Victory the *Kingdom Intercessor* Must Be Judged

The Lord calls the **Kingdom Intercessor** to come into his/her Kingdom of Heaven position as ambassador of the King of Glory and to enter into his/her position of governmental leadership. That one then chooses to trust in the name of the Lord and King Jesus Christ for victory. That one then must be prepared to receive The King as the one who judges as well as delivers out of the hand of the enemy.

God identifies himself over and over in the book of Malachi as a God who judges. In the book of Malachi, God's word comes to His followers, a people who honored God with their words, but this honor was not reflected in their lives. He warned them of His judgment. It is written…

> *"…I have no pleasure in you, saith the LORD of hosts, neither will I accept an offering at your hand."* Malachi 1:10b

If a **Kingdom Intercessor** has been proclaiming the name of the Lord as his/hers for some time and has departed from His perfect way, perhaps that is the reason for that one's defeat and failure. That one can now run to the Lord of Hosts who judges His intercessors.

It is written...

"For the priest's lips should keep knowledge, and they should seek the law at his mouth: for he is the messenger of the LORD of hosts.

"But ye are departed out of the way; ye have caused many to stumble at the law...

"Therefore have I also made you contemptible and base before all the people, according as ye have not kept my ways, but have been partial in the law." Malachi 2:7-9

    Victory may come to the **Kingdom Intercessor** even though the fullness of judgment has not been meted out to that one, but the **Kingdom Intercessor** needs to stop and let the Lord judge him/her. That one should allow the Lord to reveal that with which the Lord is displeased. As surely as the Lord reveals it, just as surely will He forgive and deliver. That one can know that his judgment may bring chastisement, but it is written...

"...My son, despise not thou the chastening of the Lord, nor faint when thou art rebuked of him:

"For whom the Lord loveth he chasteneth, and scourgeth every son whom he receiveth.

"If ye endure chastening, God dealeth with you as with sons; for what son is he whom the father chasteneth not?" Hebrews 12:5b-7

For sure deliverance, the End-time **Kingdom Intercessor** needs to cry for mercy and stay upon the Lord of Hosts for he will surely deliver. It is written...

> "*...I am in a great strait: let us fall now into the hand of the LORD; for his mercies are great: and let me not fall into the hand of man.*" II Sam. 24:14

The **Kingdom Intercessor** who comes unto the Lord of Hosts will step into a place where the enemy will have **no control over him/her** because the battle would be no longer his/hers, but the Lord's. The name of the Lord of Hosts is Jesus, and when one runs into that name, then that name becomes his/her high tower unto which one can run and be safe. That one can then know that...

> "*This is a faithful saying, and worthy of all acceptation, that Christ Jesus came into the world to save sinners...*" I Timothy 1:15

When the End-time **Kingdom Intercessor** reaches maturity, he/she shall overcome at last. That one will know that **Jesus** is now the great deliverer. That one can run quickly and confidently to the King of Heaven and commit him/herself to this King anew. One positions oneself to always look to Jesus for victory. He/she commits to the scriptures to be always...

> "*Looking unto Jesus the author and finisher of our faith; who for the joy that was set before him endured the cross, despising the shame, and is set down at the right hand of the throne of God.*" Hebrews 12:2

Whatever the enemy has put upon the mature *Kingdom Intercessor*, or put in the pathway of the mature *Kingdom Intercessor*, the Lord of Hosts stands ready to deliver. He may judge, but He will deliver His own out of the hand of the enemy. It is written...

> "...if any man sin, we have an advocate with the Father, Jesus Christ the righteous:" I John 2:1

Because Jesus, the King of the Kingdom of Heaven is Lord of Hosts, the Lord who delivers and who judges is the one whose judgment is inextricably interwoven into victory. The believer should be not afraid, though, to give up the struggle and run to Him. It is written...

> "...this man, because he continueth ever, hath an unchangeable priesthood.
>
> "Wherefore he is able also to save them to the uttermost that come unto God by him, seeing he ever liveth to make intercession for them." Heb. 7:24-25

The *Kingdom Intercessor* Called to Governmental Leadership

The End-time *Kingdom Intercessors'* call to governmental leadership is not a small, insignificant call. It is a call for a special ministry for stratospheric warfare in the heavenlies. It is a call to raise up an army of invincible soldiers for the Kingdom of Heaven on earth, ready and prepared for battle to destroy the enemy of the Church and all that works against the heritage of the Lord.

The End-time *Kingdom Intercessors* will be a special breed of leaders. The *Kingdom Intercessors* will be leaders, prepared to follow the Spirit of the Lord—they will be the prepared armies for the Lord. The *Kingdom Intercessor* leader will be totally dependent on the Holy Spirit and will have learned to hear from the Lord and will do only what the Lord directs.

The mature *Kingdom Intercessor* will know the secrets of and the power in intercessory prayer. The *Kingdom Intercessor* will know their assignment and will stay with the assignment at all cost. The End-time *Kingdom Intercessors'* army will consist of troops, and in its ranks will be prepared generals, captains, lieutenants, sergeants, and foot soldiers. Some will provide a prayer covering through stratospheric prayer warfare.

The *Kingdom Intercession* ministry will be made up of strike forces or special forces of soldiers--of ministry leaders, worshippers, intercessors--organized for special activity, fighting to win big for the King of Glory. They will defeat the wiles of the enemy, because the Holy Spirit will be their leader and constant companion.

The mature *Kingdom Intercessor* will be trained in the Spirit, by the Spirit, and through the Spirit. The ministry of *Kingdom Intercession* is a ministry for believers in Jesus Christ; that is, prepared ministers, intercessors, and all types of leaders. The Kingdom of Heaven is at hand. These End-time *Kingdom Intercessors* will be ambassadors for the King to open the way for His return.

These trained *Kingdom Intercessor* governmental leaders will be prepared for stratospheric warfare not only over and for the Church of Jesus Christ, but also for stratospheric warfare over cities, states, regions, nations, businesses, and organizations—over all that belongs to the King in order to establish the Kingdom of Heaven on earth.

WHO IS CALLED TO THE MINISTRY OF END-TIME *KINGDOM INTERCESSION*?

A clarion call issues forth from the throne of God for the End-time *Kingdom Intercessors* to come forth for the End-time ministry of *Kingdom Intercession*. This call is a call to prepare for intercession—to prepare for war. This call is being issued to every born-again believer in Jesus Christ, whether that one has had in depth ministry training. This call is a call to intercession first, last, and always. Intercession opens the way to begin, to maintain, and to end what needs to be ended. This call is issued to the following:

1. Pastors and ministry leaders with established ministries who are ready to drive the enemy out of that which God has ordained for His (God's) purposes and take dominion for the Lord.

2. Worshippers ready and/or prepared for battle.

3. Intercessors who are ready to be trained to give all to the battle.

4. Believers who love the Lord Jesus Christ and want to do something more than just attend Church and are willing to be trained for a deeper depth with Jesus and for kingdom work.

5. Believers who know they have a call for a special work, perhaps have been called to intercession, but no one has helped activate that call.

Finally, the call is for the saints/believers to enter into that great call of ***Kingdom Intercession*** to open the way for the Kingdom of Heaven to come on earth. The Kingdom must then prepare self for the fierce battle ahead. The Lord, therefore, calls for the End-time ***Kingdom Intercessor*** to come forth to attack, to overcome the enemy, to invade the enemy's territory where the enemy is entrenched, to gather together and gang up on the enemy, and to win the End-time battle in the heavenlies. Many will be called, but few will be chosen.

Additional books by Dr. Pernell H. Hewing which deal specifically with Kingdom Intercession are:
The Tribe of Israel, Judah
The Tribe of Israel, Reuben
The Tribe of Israel, Benjamin
The Tribe of Israel, Simeon
Tribe of Asher
The Tribe of Israel, Gad
(The other Tribes of Israel being edited at this writing)

KINGDOM INTERCESSORS' PRACTICAL EXERCISE

DIRECTIONS: The following practical exercise is for those who are serious about the call to prepare for the battle ahead. Preparation will require disciplined Word study and prayer. It will require spending approximately 30 minutes at least two or three times a week and a commitment to spend this time quietly with the Lord engaged in serious study, prayer and waiting before the Lord to be sanctified in the *Kingdom Intercessor* Ministry of Deliverance

For the more serious and/or more desperate, a daily study is recommended. Use the following guidelines in your study.
KEEP YOUR PRAYER NOTEBOOK AVAILABLE AND MAKE NOTES AS THE LORD GIVES REVELATION

Read and reread information from this book several times.

Prayerfully study and meditate on scriptures from Malachi and Ephesians.

*Begin your study by reading the book of Malachi as follows:

WEEK 1: Read the book of Malachi through this week. Pray before and after each reading for understanding. Pray earnestly asking the Lord to examine your life. Make notes in your prayer book of any revelation for repentance and changes you must make.

WEEK 2: Read and meditate on Malachi Chapter One each time you meet with the Lord this week. Make notes in your prayer book of any revelation for repentance and change on your part.

WEEK 3: Read and meditate on Malachi Chapter Two. Pray and meditate upon Chapter Two asking the Lord to examine your life to determine if there is anything in your life that you need to repent of and change because of the message in that chapter.

WEEK 4: Read and meditate on Malachi Chapter Three. Follow the same procedure as in Malachi One and Two.

WEEK 5: Read and meditate on Malachi Chapter Four. Pray in the Spirit. Ask the Lord to open the message of this chapter for you.

CHAPTER 12

THE END-TIME *KINGDOM INTERCESSORS* MUST OVERCOME ANCIENT DEMONIC FORCES

Ancient demonic forces are at work in the earth and are positioned to overcome the believers in Jesus Christ and destroy anything that belongs to Him. They are satan's strong ambassadors to destroy God's people and God's work **Kingdom Intercessors** must fight and destroy these ancient forces.

Ancient gods are higher than the strongholds fought earlier in self, culture, and the church. They are of higher rank and are the ones who are behind all the strongholds and all wickedness in the earth and in the Church. These are ancient gods cause havoc in the Church and in people. These ancient gods and goddesses are mentioned briefly in scripture, but as the ***Kingdom Intercessor*** comes in close to the Lord, He will reveal them and uncover them for the ***Kingdom Intercessor*** to see and defeat.

Sometimes ancient deities are mentioned so briefly in scripture that one may miss them, but they are not hidden from the King, and He will reveal them to His mature, prepared Intercessor. The Babylonian god/goddess mentioned in Isaiah 65:11 defy the living God.

It is written ...

"But ye are they that forsake the LORD, that forget my holy mountain, that prepare a table for that troop, and that furnish the drink offering unto that number." Isaiah 65:11

Isaiah 65:11 will be highlighted here to note an ancient god and an ancient goddess that wreak havoc in the Church and destroy God's people. The words in Isaiah 65:11 appear to be a general word of rebuke to Israel, but this scriptures reveals ancient gods as ruling forces against the Lord. When one examines the meaning of these names and the detrimental work of these two adversaries sent by satan, one may note that they defy what and who God is. The name *"troop,"* is a Babylonian god of fortune and is the god who is *"distributor of fortune or wealth."*[1]

This idol is a false God or a demonic power sent to control the distribution of wealth and fortune and does his greatest damage in the church and against God's people by holding back the wealth and controlling fortune. The name *"number"* is a "Babylonian goddess. She is often referred to as the Moon Goddess and is referred to in scripture as the queen of Heaven."[2] She is set to thwart the destiny of God's people and the Church of the Living God.

As long as these two ancient gods, or any ancient god, stay seated in one's life and in the Church, God's work is hindered, and His eternal purpose thwarted. These deities are defying the living God, and **Kingdom Intercessors** will be as David when Goliath defied Israel's army. It is to take…

> *"…away the reproach from Israel? for who is this uncircumcised Philistine, that he should defy the armies of the living God?"* I Samuel 17:26

---

[1] Hamon, Jane, **The Cyrus Decree**, Christian International Family Church, Santa Rosa Beach, Florida, 2003, p185

[2] Ibid, page 186

These and other ancient dieties are set to defy the purposes of the living God. The call to the *Kingdom Intercessor* is to arise in the Spirit of David as David when he met Goliath. The battle for the *Kingdom Intercessor* is no small scrimmage. They are called to prepare to uncover and confront high-level demonic powers that are defying the Living God as Goliath was.

There are many demonic powers defying the work and the ministry of God; therefore, the *Kingdom Intercessors* must come forth prepare themselves so that the Lord can trust them to route out these demonic forces. The King will reveal them to the *Kingdom Intercessor* who has met the requirement for *Kingdom Intercession*.

The *Kingdom Intercessor* may want to avoid the battle with ancient deities, but they must not because these dieties are arch enemies of the Church and the believer/saints. The End-time *Kingdom Intercessors*, therefore, must rise and prepare well. God has set the work of the church for this day. Healing and deliverance were the order of the day for the church for many years. The purpose was to prepare soldiers to stand in the heat of the battle.

Five-Fold Ministers called to *Kingdom Intercessor*

The Five-Fold Ministries established the Body in complete order, and the preparation for *Kingdom Intercession* was established as the Five-Fold ministers were established in office. The call to the office of the Five-fold Ministries was a strategic plan of God for His Divine purposes because Five-Fold Ministers are the Vanguard of *Kingdom Intercession*. They are the ones called to *Kingdom Intercession* because if one is walking in a Five-Fold office, that one was prepared by God. The preparation, therefore, for the Five-Fold office was the beginning preparation for *Kingdom Intercession*.

If one is walking in a Five-Fold Office, that one is a prepared *Kingdom Intercessor*. The preparation of the Five-Fold Ministers was preparation to prepare for *Kingdom Intercession* and to prepare End-time *Kingdom Intercessors*. These prepared and trained ones are positioned to overcome false dieties in the Church?

Five-Fold Ministers Prepared to be the End-Time Kingdom Intercessors

Ancient gods and goddesses have surely overcome the Church; therefore, it is time that the End-time *Kingdom Intercessors* sign up for battle and get ready to overcome these demonic structures in the Church. Five-Fold ministers are called to sign up for the ministry of *Kingdom Intercession*, or expect to be drafted.

Too long have the believer saints fought to overcome the demonic forces in their life and the ministers worked to help the saint/believers overcome the unholy forces which hindered them. There was a time for that ministry to and for the people, but the purpose of that was to prepare a people to overcome the enemy of the Church. When the End-time *Kingdom Intercessors* overcome the ancient deities in the Church, the Church will come forth triumphant

The prepared and trained Five-Fold *Kingdom Intercessor* will, of necessity, enter battle and go for the ruling force, the one who gives the orders and initiates the strategies of defeat of God's people and the Church. The

Five-Fold ministers must be prepared to be true **Kingdom Intercessors**. They must come forth in the spirit of David for this feat and use the wisdom of David. They must learn war and war strategies from the King. They will know war strategies because of the battles they have fought and won.

David did not wear the armor the King provided nor use the weapons of war they were using. David used unconventional weapons and rejected the usual armor. It is written...

> "...And David said unto Saul, I cannot go with these; for I have not proved them. And David put them off him.
>
> "And he took his staff in his hand, and chose him five smooth stones out of the brook, and put them in a shepherd's bag which he had, even in a scrip; and his sling was in his hand: and he drew near to the Philistine." I Samuel 17:39-40

Kingdom Intercessors **Need New Weapons of War for the Battle Ahead**

The Lord has been releasing new truths about weapons of war for this battle in the Heavenlies. At first these weapons may seem so contrary to what is being used in warfare in the Church today, but the secret of **Kingdom Intercession** and all that is about it is in the heart of God. When David faced Golaith, all of Israel and the army of Israel were standing by not knowing what to do. David faced Golaith with a most unusual weapon, a sling slot.

It appears that the Lord is providing spiritual weaponry for the End-time **Kingdom Intercessor** to use against *the enemies of the Church.* Also it seems that God has stepped on the scene to insure the End-time *Kingdom Intercessor* will move into his/her Eternal Purpose. God is, therefore, raising up the *Kingdom Intercessor* fully equipped with Kingdom-inspired spiritual armor to win the End-time Battle of the Age over the Church and to deliver the Church out of the hands of satan. It is written...

> *"The LORD hath opened his armoury, and hath brought forth the weapons of his indignation: for this is the work of the Lord GOD of hosts in the land of the Chaldeans."*
> Jeremiah 50:25

If one is ready to enter into the ministry of *Kingdom Intercession*, the Lord is introducing his weaponry from heaven for *Kingdom Intercession*. He is saying that now is the hour for the Church to be liberated from the arm who wields the weapons against the Church and the ruling forces who set the strategies. These enemies thwart the eternal purpose of God's people and the Church. When the battle is over, the Kingdom will come on earth as it is in heaven.

The mature prepared *Kingdom Intercessors* will be the ministry leaders, pastors, apostles, prophets, teachers, ministers, and scribes in the Kingdom. These End-time *Kingdom Intercessors* will then establish Kingdom ministries to open the way for the Kingdom of Heaven to come on earth, and they will be become heads of the people, and will execute judgment and the justice of the Lord.

Finally, this is a call to choose the highest call in the Kingdom. This is a call to intercession first, last, and always. It is a call to **Kingdom Intercession**. The End-time **Kingdom Intercessor** is at the forefront of the End-time Battle of the Age. It is a Royal Battle for self and for the Church. Many are called, but the one called to **Kingdom Intercession** is called because that one is called to fight the battle of the ages for self, for the Church, and all that pertains to God.

COVENANT AGREEMENT

Are you ready and willing to lay down your life and prepare for the battle of the Lord? If you are ready to lay aside the weights and sin which easily beset, stop fighting and struggling and striving, and give all up to Jesus, read and pray the following prayer and sign it as a commitment to Jesus.

*"Lord, I am tired. I am worn out, and I want and need your rest. I come to you now and choose to commit myself to you totally. I ask forgiveness of my sins and stand before you for your mercy and grace. I commit myself today to you to move and live, and have my being in you, which is living in The Covenant of Grace which I am in with you, to be trained and prepared for battle and to enter into the **Kingdom Intercessor** Ministry of Deliverance.*

"I commit myself to living by faith, to living in the light of the fact of the grace of God, and to following the Holy Spirit and to learning to depend upon the Holy Spirit....

"...in which I have access and now stand ... knowing and believing that every thing and any thing that I will ever need is made available to me through Jesus Christ and that the Holy Spirit will lead me and guide me with His eyes upon me This is the new walk I commit myself to, dear Lord. Please help me to enter into it and become established in this walk."

Name _____ Date _____

Practical Exercises

READ, PRAY, AND MEDITATE ON ISAIAH 65 AND EZEKIEL 36

Gad, the "troop" and Meni, the "number" are ancient Babylonian god and goddess. Light reading and praying will not uproot them. Set yourself to spend time praying and warring against the demonic forces. One must not only fight for self, but fight to uproot them from bloodlines.

The following scriptural prayers, confessions and declarations are suggested to help.

Scriptural Prayers and Declarations

Confessions of Faith in the Blood of Jesus

Because of the shed blood of Jesus, I am created for shared dominion with God on earth.

I choose to cast off all attitudes of failure and fear and walk in faith.

The faith I walk in is what the Word says about Jesus Christ, and about the power in His shed blood. I will believe what the Word says and confess what the Word says.
The Word says that I am justified freely by GOD'S grace through the redemption that is in Christ Jesus.

I, therefore, say that I am justified freely by God's grace through the redemption that is in Christ Jesus.

Whom God has set forth to be a propitiation through faith in his blood...

The Word is on my tongue. I speak the word over my heart, mind, body, and soul. The cleansing power of the blood delivers me from all influence of Gad, the "troop," and Meni, the "number." I am healed of all your abrasions

The Word was made flesh and the Word is the power of God. It is through the blood that Jesus Christ the mediator of the New covenant mediates for me....

For the life of the flesh is in the blood and it has been given to me upon the altar to make an atonement for my soul, for it is the blood of Jesus that maketh an atonement for my soul.

That atonement is the power of the anointing which will set me free of any influence and the workings of Gad, the "troop, and Meni, the "number." I have a covenant with the one whose blood was shed, the one who is the mediator of that new covenant.

Not by might, but by the power of the blood of Jesus will seeds of unrighteousness planted by Gad, the "troop" and Meni the "number." wither and die.

Because of the power wrought by Christ when he entered into the holy place by his own blood and obtained eternal redemption for me, my soul will be delivered from the seeds of iniquity.

Because of the power wrought by Christ when he entered into the holy place by his own blood and obtained eternal redemption for me, I am free to loose the wealth God has ordained for me, and enter into my Eternal Purpose.

Because of the power in the blood of Jesus, I am cleansed of the damage which Gad the "troop" and Meni the "number" have caused in my life.

The Power is in the Blood Covenant

I am in covenant with Jesus Christ, and He will water the seeds of righteousness that have been planted in my heart by the Word of God. I will use those words to declare my fortune is coming, my Eternal Purpose is secure.

Because the soul, or life, is in the blood, and because the blood was offered to God on the altar, it has redemptive power. That redemptive power redeems me from the work of Gad, the "Troop" in my life and also Meni the "Number."

Jesus Christ by has own blood entered in once into the Holy place having obtained eternal redemption for us.

Where iniquity has held me—my own iniquity and bloodline iniquities—I pull down those strongholds, I come up out of them. My wealth, my fortune, my Eternal Purpose is in the hands of the Almighty God.

Gad, the "troop" must let go of his control over my money, riches, and wealth, and Meni, the "number" must bow to the Jesus the Christ and bow out of my life.

Where Gad, the "troop" and Meni the "number" have held the seeds of righteousness planted in me when I received Jesus Christ, by the blood of Jesus, iniquity will let go of the seeds of righteousness
Seeds of righteousness replace seeds of iniquity in my heart.

I have much seeds of the word of righteousness in my heart. I announce that the seed of righteousness spring forth as my righteousness in Jesus Christ comes forth. Then Gad the "troop" and Meni the "number" must let go their control.

I say to the Eternal Spirit "unite with the eternal blood and come unlock my fortune, my future, and my Eternal Purpose. Righteousness will overrule the work of Gad, the "troop" and Meni, the "number."

Righteousness will spring up and overrule the seed they planted in me by the works of Gad, the "troop," and Meni, the "number."

Blood overrules. I call for the increase.

I call forth an increase in fortune and in what is needed for me to fulfill my Eternal Purpose.

My heart will open up and receive new truth–seeds of truth that will come up and prosper for me and in me.

I speak it forth not by my might and worth, but by the shed blood of Jesus Christ which flows from a fountain opened in heaven to cleanses sin and uncleanness and to destroy the work of darkness.

My conscience is cleansed from the unrighteousness sown into my heart by the enemy by the blood of Christ who through the Eternal Spirit offered himself without spot to God to purge my conscience.

My conscience is cleansed from lies planted by Gad, the "troop" and Meni, the "number."

My conscience is cleansed from the unrighteousness sown into my heart and my life by the enemy.

By the blood of Christ, I am free to serve God without fear and in holiness all the days of my life. It is written...

"As he spake by the mouth of his holy prophets, which have been since the world began:

"That we should be saved from our enemies, and from the hand of all that hate us;

"To perform the mercy promised to our fathers, and to remember his holy covenant:" Luke 1:70-72

Through the shed blood of Jesus, I am redeemed from the work of Gad, the "troop" and Meni, the "number."

The power of the blood is in the fact that it is offered to God on the altar for redemption.

I am shifting my heart to faith in the blood of Jesus who was sent forth to be a propitiation for my sin.

He was sent to declare his righteousness for the remission of sins that are past through the forebearance of God.

I declare through faith in the blood of Jesus—not faith in myself and what I know, or what I can accomplish, or what I can do, but faith in the shed blood of Jesus-the King–that I will move and speak as he moves and speaks.

I speak to the mountain of lies about who I am and what I can do, and who can stop me and what can stop me and say.

I am washed in the blood, and I can do all things through Christ who strengthens me. The power of the blood is against the working of Gad the "troop" and Meni the "number" in my life.

I speak the word of faith. Through faith in the blood of Jesus, I can do all things in Christ who strengthens me.

The wonderful power of the blood is especially manifested on behalf of sinners on earth who are saved by his grace. I am saved by grace.

For by grace are we saved through faith; and that not of ourselves: It is the gift of God.

Because of the shed blood of Jesus, I strip off the beggarly garments of weakness and timidity, but I put on the robe of righteousness of the King Jesus Christ who washed me from my sin in his own blood and hath made me king and priest unto God and his father. To him be glory and dominion forever.

I declare that through the shed blood of Jesus Christ, the altars held in place in my heart and mind by the whispers of satan and the lies of Gad the "troop" and Meni the "number" will fall.

I speak to my heart, my mind, my soul, and say, I am destined for greatness by the life blood of Jesus Christ with whom I am in blood covenant.

It was by the Eternal Spirit in our Lord that His blood had its value and power.

Through the Eternal Spirit, the blood possesses living power in Heaven, and that living power will work in my heart, mind, body and soul, to deliver and to cleanse me from the unrighteous working of Gad the "troop" and Meni the "number" in my life.

It is the living power of the blood that will uproot the altar of Gad the "troop" and Meni the "number" in my heart and life.
It is through the living power of the blood that will uproot the altar of stubbornness and rebellion.

It is through the living power of the blood that the Holy Spirit will uproot altars of lies in me.

It is through the living power of the blood through the Eternal Spirit that frees me from self, from rejection of God, from weakness and fear.

I declare that through the power of the blood, I am cleansed and sanctified to Jesus who through the Eternal Spirit offered Himself without spot to God to unite me to God.

I choose to fix my eyes on Jesus and trust in the power of His shed blood and cast off fear and failure. I align myself with Jesus and come out of agreement with Gad, the "troop" and Meni, the "number."

I am coming forth from the bottom of the hill where I have been pushed down by Gad, the "troop" and Meni, the "number." I am coming forth through the eternal blood which speaks from heaven for me.

I have the boldness to enter all the Lord Jesus died for and I enter in by the blood of Jesus,

I enter into my blessings and into my Eternal Purpose by the blood of Jesus. I come through the new and living way, which he hath consecrated for us through the veil, that is to say, his flesh:

I come to the "...high priest over the house of God." I come to Christ the high priest because...

"...Christ as a son over his own house; whose house are we, if we hold fast the confidence and the rejoicing of the hope firm unto the end." Hebrews 3:6

I come boldly with faith that the Eternal blood will speak from Heaven for me. I will arise and come forth through the blood. I will come through the new and living way which was consecrated for me through the veil of his flesh.

I come to the high priest over the household of God.

I will be blessed, because I am in a blood covenant with the high priest over the household of God.

I am coming to my hill of blessing, pushing back, tearing down the altars of Gad the "troop" and Meni the "number" that satan has had them to erect in my life to hold back my blessing.

The God of peace brought again from the dead our Lord Jesus, that great Shepherd of the sheep, through the blood of the everlasting covenant. I am in covenant with the Shepherd of the sheep.

I have access to the power of the blood of Jesus because of my covenant relationship with the Shepherd of the sheep.

Because of the wonderful person whose blood was shed, that blood has power to redeem my soul from the clutches of the enemy where iniquity has held me.

I call forth the power of the blood to wash away the altar erected in my heart by Gad the "troop" and Meni the "number." These altars of guilt and self condemnation must go. In the name of Jesus the Christ, I tear down altars of insecurity, inferiority, lies, hate, bitterness in my heart.

I speak to the altars of satan that have given off occult powers to keep me from my wealthy place and to thwart my Eternal Purpose. Your altars will fall because of the blood of atonement.

The blood of atonement has the power to redeem me from fear, from failure and open the way for me to enter my wealth place and fulfill my Eternal Purpose.

That blood has the power to accomplish everything in me that salvation accomplishes.

Now because of the shed blood of Christ, and because He has named us kings and priests unto God and his father, to Him be glory and dominion forever and ever.

I can share dominion with Christ on earth because according to the Word of God, I have been made a King and priest unto God forever and I can now be saved from my enemies, and from the hand of all that hate me, being delivered out of the hand of my enemies.

Before continuing, read the book, "The Tribe of Israel, Gad," by Pernell H. Hewing.

BOOKS BY

PERNELL H. HEWING, Ph.D., Th.D.

INTERCESSION

Calling Forth the Bride of Christ for Intercession

A treatise on the Calling, the Stripping, the Clothing, the Adorning, and the Warfare of the Bride of Christ.

This book issues a call to the reader to come into the high place of honor the Lord wills for every born-again believer--the bridal chamber of the Lord. The book presents practical exercises which leads one along the pathway to intimacy with the Lord which only the bride of Christ in intercession attains.

The Royal Priesthood, Made According to God's Plan

An Intercessory Prayer and Word Training Manual designed to lead one into deeper depths of Prayer and to prepare Intercessors, Prayer Group Leaders, and Ministers for greater Kingdom work. (CDs Available)

The Inner Court Ministry with Christ,
The Master/Teacher in the School of Prayer

This book calls every believer to the Inner Life, a Hidden Life, spent dwelling in the presence of the Lord with Christ in the School of Prayer. The Ministry of the Inner Court prepares one for powerful kingdom work undergirded with powerful, priestly prayer. The book leads one into consecrated prayer for healing of the soul, the mind, heart and the Spirit.

The Call to Adonai, Your Lord and Master And to the Bondslave Experience

This book leads a believer to lay his/her life on the altar and take up the mantle of intercession. It leads one to a complete surrender, then to birth in his/her ministry, and onto a life of continuous abiding before the Lord so that all the intercessor does is ordered by the Lord.

The Ministry of the Mizpeh Covenant

This book focuses on the truth of the meaning of covenant-making and preparing for battle. It calls one to give up idols one must deal with. It then presents the truth of covenant-making from salvation to the covenant of grace to the purpose of covenant-making. A special feature of this book is an introductionto the cross life.

The New Sound of Zion

This is a photogenic view of End-Time Zion where the Lion of Judah resides. This book issues a call to every born-again believer in Jesus Christ to prepare for a new sound from heaven to open the way for the Lion of Judah to come. The New sound of Zion is a call to worshipers, dancers, musicians, and intercessors to choose to pay the price to release the New Sound whether it be song, dance, music or Intercession to open the way for the Lion of Judah to roar in the Church

The Hebron Ministry...A Ministry of Faith, Rest, and Refuge
This book leads one to and gives meaning to going wholehearted with God. The End-Time Believer enters into Faith and REST as God ordains. When one goes wholehearted with God, the Believer will find refuge with Him.

El Shaddai
The believer who enters into this ministry will receive new life, revival, restoration and "The Blessing". The believer will understand how much he/she is in need of a blessing, if that one missed out on the "Family Blessing" during childhood. This book also leads to the healing of the wounded spirit, awakening of the sleeping spirit, and release of the imprisoned spirit.

HEALING

The Healing Streams of Bethesda
This a call to a place of healing--a place to enter into the waters of life. The message of this book points one to the healer, Jesus Christ. A special focus is placed on the three keys of healing: the grace of faith, the grace of hope, and the grace of love.

Come to Gilgal for Circumcision of the Heart
This book is the treatise of the message in Joshua 1-6 relating it to the need for circumcision of the heart for a deeper walk with God. It deals with putting an end to wilderness wandering after salvation and entrance into a sure covenant with God for Intercession for the family. (CDs Available)

The Ministry of Jehovah Rapha with Concepts of Divine Healing

In Rapha one finds healing for deep wounds, emotional scars, debilitating illness and other traumas for which many have given up hope. The Lord comes unto us in Rapha to heal not only the body, but also heals the soul and spirit.

MINISTRY

Getting to Know the Holy Spirit and Preparing for Holy Ghost Baptism with Fire

This book is written for the purposes of pleading with the believer to seek for all what was promised and to be satisfied with nothing less than full power from on high. A special focus of this book is Baptism with Holy Ghost Pentecostal fire and preparation to work the works of God in power.

Practical Aspects of the Body of Christ and the Five-Fold Ministries for the Kingdom

A deep study of the Body of Christ and Five-Fold Ministry and the various aspects of the ministry with attention being given to the call and qualifications needed to move in the varied and different offices for End-time Ministries.

The End-Time Call for Spiritual Mentoring, Teaching, Training, Fathering, Mothering, to Apostolic Covering

This book explains the different assignments God gives His servants for another's life i.e. mentoring, teaching, training, spiritual parenting (which sometimes includes natural reparenting) to Apostolic covering. Also included is special information on armour bearing;

Shiloh El-Beth-el, Calling Believers in Christ...
...in Preparation for the Ministry of the Kingdom of Heaven

Shiloh El-Beth-el is representative of the Kingdom of Heaven – the Kingdom of God on earth. It brings into focus God's ways of dealing with mankind and how it establishes His plan and purpose for and with mankind. It takes one back to the first church in the wilderness and to the Levitical Ministry of the Old Testament.

Shammah, the Ministry of the Prophet/Intercessor and of God'sProphetic People

This is a book to help the believer understand the office of the prophet/prophetess, prophecy, and this end-time prophetic movement. The messages also focus on the life and calling of the Prophet Intercessor.

MINISTRY INTERCESSION

Spiritual Authority: Understanding and Submitting to Spiritual Authority Brings Power, Authority, and Anointing

This book presents a microscopic view of Spiritual Authority in and for the Ministry and the facets of Spiritual Authority often overlooked or not known by those who *"... walked not after the flesh but after the spirit."* **Romans 8:4b**. This book helps one to understand how to enter into and walk in the authority of the believer and how to receive
and walk in the anointing.

Repentance and Remission for Entrance into Kingdom Apostolic Work

This is a book of practical exercises to prepare one for the ultimate Kingdom ministry of remitting sins. The Purpose is to take the reader on a journey of forgiveness, Holy Ghost repentance, and remission of sins for one self. It is at the end of the journey that one is prepared for Kingdom ministry.

DELIVERANCE

Smashing the Influence of Tap-Root Bondages

This book focuses on smashing the influence of the tap-root bondages of pride, rejection, rebellion, stubbornness, disobedience, and fear. It is designed to prepare one for intercession by leading one into deeper revelations of these areas in their own lives in which Satan has them bound.

*The Call to the Ministry of Deliverer Jesus Christ
Jehovah-Sabaoth*
The purpose of this book is to issue a call to the "called out" people of God to look together into the Word of God to find answers. The ministry of Sabaoth is for those who have come to the end of their strength and need deliverance—Jehovah-Sabaoth meet failure and offers deliverance.

PERSONAL GROWTH

In the Garden with the Risen Savior
This book is for anyone seeking a life centered in Christ or is already anchored in Christ. It reveals how close God can be to His own whether one trusts Him completely or whether one accepts His love, His kindness,
His forgiveness.

*Bring your Life to Divine Order
Through Two Forty-Day Consecrations*
Presenting consecrations of fasting, travailing prayer, physical cleansing, and spiritual cleansing in preparation for unconditional surrender. This book presents guidelines for two 40-day consecrations for unconditional surrender. The first is a consecration of fasting, travailing prayer, cleaning, and putting the physical environment in order. The second is a consecration in prayer and the Word of God which leads to spiritual cleansing.

Into the Depths with Jesus
The writer captures the heart of God as she records His messages for the work of the Kingdom. An account of one person's journey with God, this book speaks to all who are seeking a deeper walk with God.

The Threefold Calvary Experiences of a Christian: New Life, Death, and Resurrection in Christ.
This book is a call to look to Calvary for New Life in Jesus Christ. The information leads one through a Gethsemane Experience to death to self and into a Bond-slave Relationship with Jesus.

The Book of Ephesians
To get the Word of God in your heart, begin with the book of Ephesians. These are the study and ministry CDs and aid for memorizing scriptures. (CD only)

From Spiritual/Financial Insolvency to Financial/Spiritual Abundance
This is not a "how-to" book to read to glean more information about finances. It is a book to change your position in Christ. This can only happen as one completes Practical Exercises as directed.

FAMILY INTERCESSION

Calling Forth the Family (Priest) Intercessor To Destroy Generational Line Curses

Guidelines for entering into a life of intercession and work of Intercession for the family. Information in this book introduces the the call to be *the Family (Priest) Intercessor* and what it takes to break the back of Satan and take family members out of his hands.

Understanding and Destroying the Power in Generational Line Curses

This book is written is such a manner that one could learn enough to enter into the call to become **the Family (Priest) Intercessor.** As you grasp the information given here and say **'yes'** to what the Lord is saying, you will enter into a depth with Jesus where Satan will not be able to touch.

Divine Exchange of Curses for Blessings

This book gives an account of the battle to release the blessings in the family bloodline. It is the opposite of breaking curses, but the battle is just as fierce for unlocking blessings in the family bloodline.

Spiritual Journey into Intercession for Families in Desperate Situations

This book provides practical guidelines for interceding for a family member or for families in desperate situations. This book also calls the one praying into the position of Family (**Priest**) Intercessor.

Restoring the Beauty of Holy Matrimony

A manual of information for Married Couples, Couples Planning Marriage, Couples Planning Reconciliation after a period of Separation, and Couples contemplating divorce, or Couples locked into a troubled marriage, and for pastors, ministers and other marriage counselors.

THE TRIBES OF ISRAEL

The Tribe of Judah

This book provides a panoramic view of the Tribe of Judah beginning with his birth in Genesis and continues on into Revelations where the Lion as the Tribe of Judah comes on the scene. This gives a detailed account of Judah's ministry as worshiper, warrior, intercessor, king and priest in the End-time Church.

The Tribe of Simeon

This book provides an all encompassing view of the Tribe of Simeon commencing with his birth in Genesis and culminating in Revelations. This book gives a detailed account of Simeon's ministry as the Sword of the Lord in the End-time Church.

The Tribe of Benjamin

This book provides an all encompassing view of the Tribe of Benjamin commencing with his birth in Genesis and culminating in Revelations. This book gives a detailed account of the ministry of the End-Time Benjamites who come to the End-Time church preaching the Gospel with power.

The Tribe of Asher

This book provides an all microscopic review of the Tribe of Asher as presented in the Old Testament, and introduces the ministry of the End-time Tribe of Asherite in the Body of Christ as the one who has died to every desire except to engage in the ministry of Prayer, Intercession and warfare. The one who has the End-time ministry of Asher chooses to spend his/her life around the throne in the bridal chamber to receive the heart of the King for the Kingdom.

The Tribe of Manasseh

Manasseh is the son of Joseph adopted by Jacob as one of his own sons. The ministry of Manasseh is the key for the Kingdom as this is the ministry which will lift the church above the healing and wholeness to healing for the nations.

The Tribe of Ephraim

Ephraim is the second son of Joseph who was adopted by Jacob as one of his own. He is the one over which Jacob crossed his hand and gave him firstborn blessings although he was the second born. This book introduces the ministry of Ephraim for the Kingdom which is the one given to healing for the backsliding church.

The Tribe of Gad

The ministry of the End-time Tribe of Gad is deliverance of the church out of the hand of the enemy so that the church will be prepared for the Kingdom. This book provides the revelation that the higher purpose of the End-time Gadite ministry is to go beyond opening prison doors of the believers in Jesus Christ who are in need of deliverance, but also to deliver the church from the throes of satan and from satan's demonic infiltration.

The Tribe of Issachar

This book introduces Issachar as the Burden-bearer for the church. The End-Time Issacharite not only knows the times and seasons, but carries a ministry in for the Kingdom which encompasses one or all of the following: Intercessor, prophet, prophet intercessor, spiritual father, pastor, prayer warrior.

The Tribe of Zebulun

This book gives a historical account of the life and works of the Tribe of Zebulun in Israel and into the ministry for the Kingdom. The ministry of the End-Time Zebulunites is a Kingdom Evangelistic ministry. The Zebulun ministry will lift the church out of the four walls and open the way for a harvest to souls.

The Tribe of Dan

The ministry of the Danite in the Kingdom is multifaceted, but it begins and ends with a ministry of judgment. The Danite ministry will open the way for healing of the believer which is needed because of one missing the blessing of natural parents. The End-time Danite will be positioned in the church and the Kingdom to know and to see—Especially see and discern unholy priest/pastor/leader in the Church

The Tribe Napthtali

The Ministry of the End-Time Napthali is Prophetic Intercessor, Watchman and warrior. Napthtali is a hind let loose: he giveth goodly words. The Ministry of the Naphtali in the Kingdom is the Prophet-Intercessor in the Kingdom who has been brought into a hidden place with the Lord in order to be the hind loosed to destroy the enemy camp in and over the church.

The Tribe of Reuben

Reuben is the first son of Jacob, but did not receive his firstborn birthright. The ministry of the End-Time Reubenite is to bring the church to see the Son, Jesus Christ. As the Reubenites come on the scene in the church, eyes will be opened to see the Son, high and lifted up, calling the church up higher to enter into the Kingdom.

The Tribe of Levi

This book will lead the reader along a pathway to unconditional surrender and to live as the priest of old in order to become End-Time ministers of the Kingdom. The ministry of the End-Time Levite is the ministry of the Royal Priesthood. The signs of the times are upon the Church for the End-Time Levitical Minstry to come forth and open the way for the King to come.

Order from:
Sanctuary Word Press,
921 W. Main St., Whitewater, WI 53190-1706
Phone: (262) 473-7472 † Fax: (262) 473-9724
E-mail: hewingph@idcnet.com
Website: www.thesanctuarywhitewater.com

www.ingramcontent.com/pod-product-compliance
Lightning Source LLC
Chambersburg PA
CBHW072336300426
44109CB00042B/1645